TRANSFORMATIVE VISIONS:

Works by Haitian Artists from the Permanent Collection

Kate Ramsey and Louis Herns Marcelin

Published on the occasion of the exhibition *Transformative Visions: Works by Haitian Artists from the Permanent Collection*, November 8, 2014 – January 18, 2015.

Organized by Louis Herns Marcelin, Ph.D. and Kate Ramsey, Ph.D.

Transformative Visions was made possible by Beaux Arts and the general membership of the Lowe Art Museum, with additional support from the Linnie E. Dalbeck Memorial Foundation Trust. Additional funding was provided by the Miami-Dade County Department of Cultural Affairs, the Cultural Affairs Council, the Miami-Dade County Mayor and the Board of County Commissioners.

Programmatic support was provided by HSBC, the University of Miami's Center for the Humanities, the College of Arts and Sciences' Strategic Initiatives Fund, Caribbean Literary and Cultural Studies in the Department of English, the Department of Modern Languages and Literatures Joseph Carter Memorial Fund, the Department of Anthropology, the Department of Art and Art History, the Department of History, the Program in Africana Studies, and the Program in American Studies.

Library of Congress Control Number: 2014956250
ISBN: 978-0-9894684-3-5

Design: Catapult[13]

Catalogue photography: Daniel Portnoy

Copy-editor: Barbara Hoffmann

Translations: Patricia Bobeck and Gary M. Gluck for The Language Corner

Printing: NuPress of Miami, Inc.

Note: In dimensions, height precedes width, which precedes depth.

COVER (Catalogue No. 20):
Pascale Monnin
L'Ange de la Résurrection (Resurrection Angel), 2006-2011

INSIDE COVER (Catalogue No. 9):
Préfète Duffaut
Troisième tentation (Third Temptation), ca. 1965

INSIDE BACK COVER (Catalogue No. 10):
Edouard Duval-Carrié
Trois feuilles (Three Leaves), ca. 1998

BACK COVER (Catalogue No. 22):
Prosper Pierre-Louis
Issa, not dated

Mario Benjamin
b. 1964, Port-au-Prince, Haiti
Untitled, ca. 1996
mixed media on masonite
60 x 48 1/4 x 3 7/8 in. (152.4 x 122.6 x 9.8 cm)
Gift of Dr. and Mrs. Carl Eisdorfer, 2002.57.48

TRANSFORMATIVE VISIONS

FOREWORD

It is my distinct pleasure, as the Lowe Art Museum's new Beaux Arts Director and Chief Curator, to introduce *Transformative Visions: Works by Haitian Artists from the Permanent Collection*. This marvelous exhibition, which was conceived of and curated by University of Miami faculty members Kate Ramsey (Associate Professor, Department of History) and Louis Herns Marcelin (Associate Professor, Department of Anthropology), was drawn entirely from the Lowe's remarkable holdings of Haitian art. Designed to highlight the diversity of Haitian visual culture as well as the inter-generational, transnational dialogues that mark the relationship between Haitian and Haitian-American artists, *Transformative Visions* brings together over two dozen objects that have never before been exhibited as a cohesive group. These pieces—which were created between 1960 and 2013—shed new light on Haitian culture by challenging stereotypes and interrogating assumptions about the creation, consumption, and interpretation of art both on the island and across the diaspora. The results are *transformative* indeed.

I would like to express my deep thanks to Drs. Ramsey and Marcelin for their tireless commitment to this project, which included a stellar artists panel (moderated by Jerry Philogene and featuring Haitian artists Myrlande Constant, André Eugène, Adler Guerrier, and Pascale Monnin) in November 2014. I would also like to extend my sincere gratitude to my predecessor, Brian Dursum, who—as Director and Chief Curator of the Lowe from 1990 until 2014—actively expanded and carefully stewarded the Museum's fine Haitian collection. Additional thanks are owed to the many donors who have gifted works on view and thereby enhanced the Lowe's capacity to fulfill its commitment to serving as an invaluable resource for education and enrichment through art and culture. I am equally grateful to the donors, foundations and funding agencies without whose support this project would not have been possible, including Beaux Arts, the Miami-Dade County Department of Cultural Affairs and the Cultural Affairs Council, the Miami-Dade County Mayor and Board of County Commissioners. Additionally, I thank our general membership, whose support undergirds all our activities, and my talented colleagues at the Lowe: it is a privilege to lead such a dedicated team. The opening reception for *Transformative Visions* and *Art in Real Life* and the *Transformative Visions* Artists' Dialogue was generously underwritten by HSBC. Additional support for this engaging panel discussion was provided by University of Miami's Center for Humanities and the College of Arts and Sciences' Strategic Initiatives Fund; the College's Programs in Africana Studies and American Studies; the Departments of Anthropology, Art and Art History, and History; Caribbean Literary and Cultural Studies in the Department of English; and the Modern Languages and Literatures Joseph Carter Memorial Fund. Bacardi generously donated in-kind support for the exhibition's opening while the Interuniversity Institute for Research and Development (INURED) provided staffing and logistical support in Haiti and assisted with interviews and transcriptions as well. To them all, I say *Mèsi anpil* (thank you very much)!

Jill Deupi J.D., Ph.D.
Beaux Arts Director and Chief Curator

ACKNOWLEDGMENTS

The *Transformative Visions* exhibition and catalogue were made possible through the vision, collaboration, and support of many individuals and institutions. First, we wish to thank Brian A. Dursum and Kara Schneiderman for inviting us to work on this project, and for their contributions to its development over a year and a half. We are likewise grateful to Jill Deupi for her commitment to the full and successful realization of every dimension of the envisioned project, including a landmark opening dialogue among Haiti- and Miami-based artists. Other Lowe staff members have been supportive and guiding partners throughout the process as well. Raymond Mathews shepherded the catalogue from the early stages of conception to its publication; Natasha Cuervo, Darren Price, and Alessia Lewitt oversaw all aspects of the installation of the exhibition; Jodi Sypher was the lead organizer of the opening event and coordinated other programming around the show; Lorrie Stassun handled the many financial aspects of the project; and Julie Berlin assisted with research on the acquisition history of each work of art.

For their great contributions to this catalogue our special thanks go to Carlo A. Célius, Pascale Monnin, and Jerry Philogene. We are grateful to Katherine Mato, M. Stephanie Chancy, Jennifer Garcon, Amelia Hintzen, and Hadassah St. Hubert who wrote the catalogue entries on individual pieces. We are also indebted to Barbara Hoffmann for her consummate copy-editing. Many thanks go as well to the Behavioral and Social Science Research Center (BSSRC) for transcribing Louis Herns Marcelin's interview with Pascale Monnin. We are grateful to Patricia Bobeck and Gary M. Gluck (both of The Language Corner) for translating from the French, respectively, the Monnin interview and Célius's essay. Much of the photography in this volume is the work of Daniel Portnoy, and the catalogue was laid out and designed by Catapult [13].

For their contributions to the success of the opening Artists' Dialogue we thank first and foremost Jerry Philogene, who served as moderator, and the participating artists, Myrlande Constant, André Eugène, Adler

Guerrier, and Pascale Monnin. We are also grateful to Fedo Boyer and CreoleTrans for providing simultaneous translations during this discussion.

Many colleagues and a wide range of units at UM provided meaningful support over the course of our work on this project. For their generous co-sponsorship of the *Transformative Visions* opening dialogue we extend heartfelt thanks to the College of Arts and Sciences' Strategic Initiatives Fund; Caribbean Literary and Cultural Studies in the Department of English; the Center for the Humanities; the Department of Modern Languages and Literatures Joseph Carter Memorial Fund; the Department of Anthropology; the Department of Art and Art History; the Department of History; the Program in Africana Studies; and the Program in American Studies. We are also grateful to Dean Leonidas G. Bachas, Edmund Abaka, Traci Ardren, Donette A. Francis, Rose-Ketlie Glemaud, Karl Gunther, Jennifer Lewis, Mary Lindemann, Lillian Manzor, Perri Lee Roberts, Patricia Saunders, Mihoko Suzuki, and Nathan Timpano.

We have greatly appreciated the generous support, input, and guidance of colleagues, contacts, and friends beyond UM as well, including Edouard Duval-Carrié, Lara Stein Pardo, Katherine Smith, and Gina Athena Ulysse.

We were thrilled that the Lowe Art Museum took this opportunity to expand its collection of works by Haitian artists. It was Kara Schneiderman's inspired idea to acquire Pascale Monnin's mobile *L'Ange de la Résurrection* in honor of the retirement of Brian A. Dursum, and generous funding from the Beaux Arts of the Lowe Art Museum made this purchase possible. Our thanks go to Pascale Monnin and the Galerie Monnin for facilitating the purchase of Louisiane Saint Fleurant's *Untitled* and André Eugène's *Ayiti Pap Peri*. Leah Gordon and, of course, Eugène himself were instrumental in this latter acquisition as well. We were delighted to be able to acquire Florine Demosthene's *Assed Out* from the artist, as well as Myrlande Constant's *Points Saint Miel* with the help of Reynald Lally. Our thanks go to Brian A. Dursum for donating Clotaire Bazile's *Saint Jacques Majeur* to the Lowe in memory of Michael J. McEachen, and to Lowe Chief Security Officer Marie Milhomme, members of her family, the family of Clotaire Bazile, Rachel Beauvoir-Dominique, and Anna Wexler for facilitating this acquisition.

There are certain supporters close to us whose contributions to the project were indispensable every step of the way. Our heartfelt thanks go to Louise Marcelin; Tim Watson; and Toni Cela, Coordinator of the Interuniversity Institute for Research and Development, as well as INURED staff members Seth Spencer Guignard and Cindia M. Marcelin.

The Lowe Art Museum would like to acknowledge and thank the following donors whose gifts over the years helped to make this exhibition possible: Beaux Arts of the Lowe Art Museum; Anne Doniger; Brian A. Dursum; Dr. and Mrs. Carl Eisdorfer; Marvin Ross Friedman; Marilyn Holifield; Richard Levine; Jewel Schainack; Larue Storm; Sacha Tebó; Gonzalo and Louise Valdes-Fauli; and Dr. and Mrs. Bernard M. Wagner.

Major funding for this exhibition and catalogue is made possible through the generosity of Beaux Arts and the membership of the Lowe Art Museum with additional support from the Miami-Dade County Department of Cultural Affairs, the Cultural Affairs Council, the Miami-Dade County Mayor and Board of County Commissioners.

Kate Ramsey and Louis Herns Marcelin

While the spelling of Kreyòl words in this catalogue follows the orthography established by the Haitian government in 1979, we preserve other spellings in titles of art works and in quotations. Plural forms of nouns in Kreyòl are not indicated by a change of ending, and thus we have chosen not to add s in such cases.

TRANSFORMATIVE VISIONS: *AN INTRODUCTION*

Kate Ramsey

The Lowe Art Museum's collection of works by Haitian artists began when Sacha Tebó — an alumnus of the University of Miami — donated his painting *Le Mariage* (cat. no. 24) in 1966, an acquisition that was followed several years later by the purchase of Préfète Duffaut's *Troisième Tentation* (cat. no. 9). Since then the collection has expanded through a combination of donations and purchases, particularly under the directorship of Brian A. Dursum, who retired in 2014. While numbers of these works have been featured in other exhibitions over the years, and Edouard Duval-Carrié's *Trois Feuilles* (cat. no. 10) hangs in one of the museum's permanent galleries, *Transformative Visions* represents the first time that these pieces have been mounted together. The exhibition is thus an opportunity to find new resonances among works by major, lesser known, and emerging artists spanning over five decades.

Transformative Visions has not been curated according to a tightly focused theme or singular vision but rather draws together an array of paintings, sculptures, and textile works from the museum's larger collection. Taken together these pieces challenge reductive and stereotypic assumptions about "Haitian art," historicizing that capacious category and spotlighting the diversity and interconnection of works falling under it. Perhaps in spite of but more likely because of the exhibition's eclecticism, a set of larger questions and themes emerges from it, elucidated in different ways by the essays, interview, and entries that comprise this catalogue. As cultural anthropologists — I am also a historian and Louis Herns Marcelin directs the Interuniversity Institute for Research and Development in Port-au-Prince — we have approached the exhibition with a longstanding mutual interest in material cultures and the social life of things; the role of markets and institutions in the production of value and taste; and the construction of identity through art-making and performance. More specifically, as scholars focused on Haiti's past and present we are interested in how works of art produced by differently-positioned artists nuance, complicate, and explode particular ideas and narratives about Haiti that have long circulated internationally. *Transformative Visions* thus highlights transformation as an artistic process, theme, and also *potential* of the works featured in the exhibition and of the greater corpus of Haitian visual art.

Catalogue essays by Carlo A. Célius and Jerry Philogene focus on diverse works in the exhibition to analyze both the particularity of Haitian artistic production and its connections to wider contemporary artistic movements and currents. Célius begins his essay "Metamorphoses" by considering the ongoing significance of two decisive — and linked — turns in Haitian art history: first, the shift away from elite subjects and towards popular ones in the context of the *"indigéniste"* movement of the late 1920s and 1930s; and then, in the next decade, the emergence of subaltern painters and sculptors as among Haiti's most prominent artists and those whose work, for years, was most favored by the international art market. To this day, Célius notes, subaltern artists "continue to play a significant and central role" in Haitian artistic creation (p. 54), a point that Annie Paul reinforces in noting that Haiti along with Cuba is a place "where…art is no longer the exclusive preserve of the middle and upper classes."[1]

Both Célius and Philogene point to and reflect on the transnationalism that shapes contemporary "Haitian art" — a category that Philogene closely interrogates in her essay "Pictures from Heaven: *Transformative Visions* and Haitian Diasporic Artistic Practices." Exploring how different works in the exhibition — and their combination — challenge stereotypical preconceptions of Haitian artistic production, Philogene situates these pieces in relation to broader currents of black Atlantic visual culture. Pascale Monnin, a featured artist in the exhibition (cat. no. 20) who helps direct a longstanding gallery in Pétionville, reflects in her interview with Marcelin on the transnationalism of her own development as an artist moving between Haiti and Switzerland, as well as on what it means that the art market for work by Haiti-based artists has long been internationally dominated. If in decades past this market was sustained, in part, by the tourist trade, she notes that in times of political crisis and disaster it is more tied into waves of international intervention — "the only times when the world thinks about Haiti. This is when the journalists and humanitarians come, and while they're at it, before leaving again, visit the galleries" (p. 49).

In these texts, formal and thematic analysis of artistic works is inseparable from questions of social and cultural history, migration and diaspora, and contemporary north-south geopolitics. In the pages that follow I draw upon the ideas and arguments of catalogue contributors in considering what the Lowe's particular collection of paintings, sculptures, and textile pieces reveals about Haitian art history and contemporary artistic practice in the context of wider political, socio-economic, and cultural frames. My specific touchstones are: Célius's discussion of how Haitian artists have long drawn on and reinterpreted religious iconography in their work; Philogene's critique of the production of Haitian art as a space of exception, isolated from transnational and international currents and conversations; and, finally, Monnin's call for greater research on the artistic genealogies of Haitian artists and their interconnections — a project that seems particularly important in light of the powerful "ways of seeing" that have shaped international reception and interpretation of Haitian art since at least the 1940s.

***

Carlo A. Célius opens his essay by examining the ways in which Haitian artists have long drawn on "certain iconographic references as a resource available for transfiguration and transformation" (p. 55). In particular, he focuses on how artists since the 1940s-50s have worked with Christian imagery across diverse media. In so doing, they have also often explored how saints, angels, crosses, the Madonna, etc. are internalized in and reinterpreted through the Vodou religion. As Célius's essay foregrounds, the Lowe's collection encompasses multiple works that depict or thematize the transformative ritual practices of Vodou, making the exhibition a particularly interesting vantage point for examining the varied but iconographically interconnected ways in which artists have represented the spirits or *lwa*.

In Vodou belief and practice the human and spirit worlds are tied by bonds of reciprocity, and the "mounting" of initiates by *lwa* in the context of ceremonies enables spirits to guide, cure, comfort, correct, and otherwise communicate with those present. *Lwa* are invited by the performance of drum rhythms, songs, and dances with which they are identified; by the offering of favorite foods and drink; and also through the drawing of intricate cosmograms called *vèvè* in their honor on the ground with cornmeal. Pauleus Vital's painting *Ezili Je Wouj* (cat. no. 27) features three of these sacred designs, invoking the Petwo *lwa* Mèt Kalfou and Ezili Je Wouj. The ritual space is defined, enclosed, and centered by a towering *mapou* (silk cotton) tree whose middle limb takes on the cast of Ezili Je Wouj herself, pouring libations and clutching the whip associated with Petwo spirits.

Clotaire Bazile's *drapo* (or ritual flags) in honor of *Erzulie Freda and Dambala Ouedo* (cat. no. 2) and *Saint Jacques Majeur* (cat. no. 3), the saint associated with the *lwa* Ogou, depict these spirits in another iconographic mode. While Bazile created these flags as objects of art — the earlier one among the first that he produced for sale and the later one among the last before his tragic 2012 disappearance — ceremonial flags, historically less ornate, have long been used in ceremonies to salute and honor the *lwa*.[2] Some depict *vèvè* designs and others, like these by Bazile, feature images of the Roman Catholic saints identified with particular spirits. Mid-twentieth century anthropologists like Melville J. Herskovits made such associations the textbook case of religious "syncretism," arguing that in the context of colonial repression of African-based ritual practices, enslaved people metonymically linked Fon, Yoruba, and Kongo spirits with the saints as a kind of protective camouflage. More recently, scholars such as Karen McCarthy Brown have reinterpreted such identifications as active attempts on the part of enslaved people to appropriate and re-channel spiritual power — to perform, as she puts it, "an end run around the oppressors, a direct appeal to the gods before whom the masters knelt."[3]

After the 1804 Revolution, the Roman Catholic Church officially left Haiti for over a half century, refusing recognition to the second postcolonial nation in the hemisphere for nearly as long as the first — the United States — did.[4] Once Haiti signed a Concordat with the Vatican in 1860, the now familiar chromolithographic portraits of the saints arrived there with French Catholic clergy and, as Donald J.

Cosentino discusses, "provided common faces for all the major *lwa*," becoming "a primary source for the elaboration of Vodou hagiography."[5] As Célius notes in his essay, such iconography also became the target of ongoing Church campaigns to purge popular Catholicism of the taint of "superstition."[6]

During the late nineteenth and early twentieth centuries, fine art production in Haiti centered on landscape painting and portraiture (both painted and photographic) of historical figures and elite patrons.[7] These subjects shifted in the later years of the 1915-1934 U.S. occupation of Haiti when pathfinding ethnologist Jean Price-Mars in his 1928 *Ainsi parla l'oncle* (So Spoke the Uncle) called upon Haitian writers, composers, and artists to look to popular cultures, with Vodou at their center, as a repository of artistic inspiration.[8] Pétion Savain, who made Haitian rural life the thematic focus of his work, was the most prominent figure of the *indigéniste* turn in Haitian painting during the 1930s (illustration 1).[9] *Indigénisme* was also the informing context and

Illustration 1

Pétion Savain
b. 1906, Port-au-Prince, Haiti
d. 1975
Market on the Hill, 1938
oil on canvas
OAS | Art Museum of
the Americas Collection, Gift
of IBM

wellspring for U.S. artist DeWitt Peters's co-founding of the Centre d'Art in 1944, an event that has too often been mythologized as the birth of Haitian art from a void through the "discovery" of the work of popular painters. Thereafter Vodou ritual and the *lwa* emerged as increasingly important subjects of Haitian artistic production, a consequence of numbers of Vodouyizan becoming recognized painters (most famously, Hector Hyppolite and André Pierre), of the international art market encouraging and rewarding such work, and of a wider cross-section of artists becoming interested in the figurative possibilities of representing these spirits in painting, sculpture, textile work, etc. The originality and diversity in artists' portrayal of the *lwa* across a range of media underscore that, as Katherine Smith notes, there is "no predetermined Vodou imaginary."[10]

The Lowe's collection affords a particularly wide-ranging perspective on how prominent artists, particularly since the 1970s, have imagined the *lwa* as beings with recognizable physical forms — that is, beyond the abstraction of *vèvè* and the surrogacy of saints, and independent of their "mounting" of initiates during ceremonies. The painters associated with the Saint-Soleil art movement — initiated in the early 1970s by Jean-Claude Garoute (Tiga) and Maud Robard in the community of Soisson-la-Montagne in the hills above Pétionville — have been particularly iconoclastic, not following codified iconography in their portrayals of *lwa*, but rather often representing them as submerged in the aquatic realm beneath the earth where spirits live. Prosper Pierre-Louis's painting *Lavender Lwa* (cat. no. 21) is characteristically devoid of iconographic clues about which specific spirits are depicted, even if they are clearly differentiated from one another. The symmetrical doubling of the two figures depicted in Levoy Exil's *Untitled* (cat. no. 12) suggests that they might represent the *marasa*, or sacred twins, often invoked and honored towards the beginning of ceremonies. However, as Leah Gordon notes, to the extent that Pierre-Louis, Exil, and other Saint-Soleil artists have "[f]ollow[ed] their own personal visual rules to represent the spirits, their works are resistant to theological explication."[11]

Edouard Duval-Carrié, one of the most prominent Haitian artists working today, has been exploring what he calls the artistic "personification" of the *lwa* since at least the late 1970s, when he painted a work entitled *Azaka Agro Rex* (Azaka King of Agriculture) that became the first of a series featuring the spirit world. In a 1995 interview he remembered wishing to create "full, flesh-type of pictures so that people would readily recognize the *lwa* from their attributes."[12] Playing with identifying "keys" of costume, prop, and color, Duval-Carrié created a pantheon of mystical yet also historical *lwa*, who in his series *Milocan, ou La migration des esprits* (Milocan, or The Migration of the Spirits) are themselves forcibly migrated in chains from a lush Ginen — or mythic Africa — to a Caribbean elsewhere. The last panel of the series, *Le monde actuel, ou Erzulie interceptée* (The World at Present, or Erzulie Intercepted), features Ezili Freda detained at sea by a pair of armed coast guard officers (illustration 2).[13]

Duval-Carrié once noted, "I've always liked the re[-]creation of things. In Haiti, it is very prevalent. They recuperate things that are from the United States or Europe in their own context."[14] His triptych *Trois Feuilles* in the Lowe collection focuses on such reinterpretations and also performs a number of its own. The work is structured in the form of a massive Catholic altarpiece with cut-out windows revealing a recessed world lying just beneath the exterior wooden surfaces. The central and largest panel frames a trinity of male *lwa*: in the foreground, a muscular figure smoking a pipe, his hands raised and palms facing out, with two successively younger and slighter spirits rising behind and above him, their arms symmetrically bent and uplifted. Leaves crown their faces like dreadlocks, and they are set amidst a background of luxuriant foliage. They resemble and are positioned similarly to the three Simbi water spirits embodied in Duval-Carrié's earlier painting *Trois Fois Simbie* (1990), but here are re-contextualized in the frame of the altarpiece, surrounded by recessed openings and niches featuring bronze masks and other power objects, and flanked on either side by gilded palm trees.[15] The piece evokes the centrality of leaves in Vodou healing practices and its title more specifically cites the ritual song "Twa fèy, twa rasin" — three

Illustration 2

Edouard Duval-Carrié
*Le monde actuel, ou Erzulie
interceptée* (The World at Present,
or Erzulie Intercepted), 1996
Oil on canvas in artist's frame
Bass Museum of Art
Gift of Sanford A. Rubenstein
© 1996 Edouard Duval-Carrié

leaves, three roots — a meditation on losing and reclaiming, forgetting and remembering that has been much recorded by Haitian singers since the 1950s: "Twa fèy, twa rasin o/Jete bliye, ranmase sonje/Mwen genyen basen mwen/Twa fèy tonbe ladan/Jete bliye, ranmase sonje (Three leaves, three roots/Throw away to forget, pick up to remember/I have my pool [or basin] of water/Three leaves fell into it/Throw away to forget, pick up to remember.)"[16] Evoking histories of displacement, dislocation, exile, and loss, the song conveys that cultural remembrance and reinterpretation are active and transformative processes, ones that Duval-Carrié thematizes and also practices in this installation and in many of his other works.

In figuring these spirits within the frame of an "Old World" Catholic altarpiece, Duval-Carrié engages another theme found in works across the Lowe's collection — one that might be called the interconnection of worlds. This takes multiple forms, including representations of the physical and spiritual worlds as not just proximate but continuous. In his painting of the third temptation of Christ, Préfète Duffaut interconnects human and otherworldly realms through a labyrinthine network of roads and footpaths passing from valleys to mountains and across the skyline. Resplendent spiritual beings preside over three realms that are spatially defined and yet not removed from the busy network of travel throughout the painting. Here again Roman Catholic and Vodou iconographies become archives for artistic reinterpretation and transfiguration, and the physical interconnection of these beings and worlds through Duffaut's system of passageways is particularly striking. In interviews with Marcelin following the January 12, 2010 earthquake, Duffaut emphasized "the importance of remaking the world in harmony with the 'Beyond,'" thus reinforcing the principles of connectivity and transformation that this earlier work also explores.[17]

The living, deceased, and spirit figures in Myrlande Constant's intricately detailed, painterly *drapo Points Saint Miel* (cat. no. 7) are poised in circular motion around the *mapou* tree at the center of both the work and of the cycles of life depicted.[18] As Célius and Philogene discuss in their essays, Constant is a leading figure among a new generation of *drapo* artists, and her technical innovations enable greater narrative possibilities. According to Constant in an interview with Marcelin, the Saint Miel are a diverse group of *lwa* from both the Rada and Petwo *nanchon* (nations) of spirits who are closely involved in the communities they watch over. The Saint Miel are present as a woman gives birth on the left side of the *drapo*; as a *manbo* (female priest) ritually prepares the body of a deceased woman for burial; and are joined by Gede spirits at a gravesite on the right side of the piece.[19] Constant's tableau speaks to the bonds of reciprocity that connect families and communities with the spirit world in everyday life and at the moments of transition the *drapo* portrays.

Other works evoke Haiti's relation to places decidedly of this world but *lòt bò dlo* (on the other side of the water), and, in so doing, comment on the country's geopolitical positioning past and present, particularly in relation to the United States. Nacius Joseph's wooden sculpture *Boat People* (ca. 1982, cat. no. 16) condenses a decade of perilous migration by small crafts from Haiti under the Jean-Claude Duvalier dictatorship to the Bahamas or South Florida. Aligned one behind the other in what appears to be a long, low canoe, six passengers gaze intently forward. The central figure holds a large fish that may invoke both Saint Ulrich and Agwe, *lwa* of the seas, for protection. In creating this work Joseph was likely responding to the swelling numbers of Haitians taking to the seas in 1980-1981 as well as to the interdiction agreement that the Reagan administration signed with the Duvalier government after assuming office. This September 1981 treaty ensured that the vast majority of those fleeing the island and intercepted would be forcibly repatriated on the presumption that they were economic rather than political refugees. Joseph's work refocuses on the people driven to embark on these hazardous journeys and the uncertainties of their passage as they look ahead into the unseen and unknown. His sculpture is part of a larger field of artistic production centered on the migration of Haitians by sea — often evoking memories of the Middle Passage — and on the politics of their reception in the United States.[20]

In his *Les Séquelles de la Colonisation* (cat. no. 28), Frantz Zéphirin reflects on both the legacies of French colonialism in Haitian society and on the country's contemporary neocolonial relationship to the U.S. Characteristically, he centers his allegory on three fantastic hybrid beings — a rooster head on a human body; a mermaid in a gendarme's cap and jacket; and a double-headed ram and long-necked bird with a lobster-claw arm, and a fishtail lower body. Alligators, fish, and zebras fill the lower background of the painting. Zéphirin often makes what Célius terms metamorphosis — when "human, animal, and plant shapes meet, combine, transform and mutate to give birth to composite beings and objects" — the vehicle for his social and political commentaries (p. 63). The artist writes of this piece: "The actors of the Haitian crisis metamorphize into wild animals so as to have their piece of the cake. But in the end it is the people who suffer" while "the big neighbor [the United States] looks on at them without doing anything because in reality he is the great winner."[21]

André Eugène's work probes Haiti's relation to "other worlds" that mass-produce, consume, and discard as waste the materials with which he sculpts. Eugène is one of the most prominent of the self-identified "Atis Rezistans," the collective of sculptors who live and work on the Grand Rue in Port-au-Prince, and have in recent years become well-known for creating pieces that transform industrial detritus into figurative assemblages — "cyberpunk" emanations of the *lwa* Bawon Samdi, Gede, and Ezili for example — that interrogate masculinity, sexuality, class immobility, militarism, globalization, and Haiti's position in the geopolitical order.[22] As Philogene notes, the repurposing of such materials also indexes the boom and bust cycles of low-wage factory work, with multinational companies subcontracting through local elites. While Eugène's work along with that of other Atis Rezistans has often been described as apocalyptic and dystopic, the ethos of his recent sculpture *Ayiti Pap Peri* (cat. no. 11) departs from such visions, instead affirming survival, staying power, and regeneration in the wake of the January 2010 earthquake. Those assurances are embodied in the figure of a woman with jade-green eyes and a half-smile, her cheeks marked with bent nails, and her carved wooden head haloed with a circular metal rim, holding close to her chest an infant whose own carved head peaks out from under a gently falling aluminum coverlet. She seems to be Eugène's reimagining of the Petwo *lwa* Ezili Dantò, a strong, protective single mother who is identified both with Mater Salvatoris — likewise scarred on one cheek — as well as with Notre Dame du Perpétuel Secours, the patron saint of Haiti. In covering the devastation of the earthquake, foreign commentators referred repeatedly to the "resilience" of impoverished Haitians in the face of seemingly impossible adversity and suffering, leading novelist and essayist Edwidge Danticat to wonder if that attribution might "not in the end hurt the affected Haitians" by rationalizing a "lack of urgency or neglect."[23] With its resonances of Ezili Dantò, warrior woman and protective mother, *Ayiti Pap Peri* eschews "this much-admired resilience" in favor of a portrait of strength based in struggle, independence, and powerful parental love.

J. Michael Dash has argued that "[c]ontemporary practices of writing and reading are ultimately about restoring a new worldliness to Haitian narrative," and that recent Haitian fiction — including works by Danticat and Dany Laferrière — is "re-siting…Haitian narrative in a new relational space."[24] Dash's attention here not just to writing but also to reading seems particularly salutary, and transferable to the interpretation of Haitian visual art as well. Jerry Philogene's catalogue essay points to the new interpretive possibilities that open when Haitian art is recognized as engaged with "black Atlantic visual aesthetics and culture" as well as with wider transnational visual and performance art currents (p. 78). This recognition of the "worldliness" of Haitian artistic production and, as Donald J. Cosentino has argued, its longstanding cosmopolitanism, seems especially important in light of the refusal of such interpretations on the parts of some of the most influential twentieth century interpreters of Haitian art.[25]

Célius has analyzed elsewhere the degree to which the writings of Selden Rodman (author of the 1948 *Renaissance in Haiti: Popular Painters in the Black Republic* among other books) constructed the work of subaltern artists associated with the Centre d'Art in the later 1940s and 1950s as emerging spontaneously and in isolation from any external influence.[26] By such logic, autochthony became the guarantee of authenticity and underwrote the conclusion as well that the "intuitive" creativity of artists such as Philomé Obin and Hector Hyppolite had to be "protected" from any exposure to academicism lest their "natural" gifts be ruined. To the extent that such ideologies guided DeWitt Peters's direction of the Centre d'Art during the later 1940s, they also played a strong role in a number of artists — particularly those with formal training — breaking with the Centre d'Art to form the Foyer des Arts Plastiques in 1950, issuing a "manifesto" that began: "Haitian art, like art everywhere, cannot develop in a vacuum."[27] Yet the international popularity of the so-called *"naïf"* style of Haitian painting only seemed to deepen the foreign investment in this fantasy of art created without genealogy and independent of external influence. André Malraux, in writing about his 1975 visit to the Saint-Soleil community in Soisson-la-Montagne at Tiga's invitation, stressed again the isolation of these artists and their unfamiliarity with other forms of visual representation.[28]

From the mid-1940s on, the international reception and consumption of "Haitian art" — assumed by many to be reducible to the styles called "primitive" or, again, "naïve" — reinforced Haiti's status as a space apart, more specifically as "the magic island" after the title of W. B. Seabrook's infamous occupation-era travelogue.[29] Such a label was ambivalently affirmative but closely affiliated, as Philogene discusses, with projections of exceptionalism that constructed Haiti as aberrant and explicable only with reference to itself. As Michel-Rolph Trouillot writes in an oft-quoted passage from the influential essay that Philogene also cites: "Haitian exceptionalism has been a shield that masks the negative contribution of the Western powers to the Haitian situation. Haitian exceptionalism functions as a shield to Haiti's integration into a world dominated by Christianity, capitalism, and whiteness. The more Haiti appears weird, the easier it is to forget that it represents the longest neocolonial experiment in the history of the West." The mystification of Haiti as a place unlike any other — whether this was seen as cause for celebration or derision — has meant that Haitian society "escapes analysis and comparison" and that by extension there is nothing that Haiti can teach the rest of world.[30] Lamentably, as Sibylle Fischer and others have examined, foreign construction of Haiti as a space of exception and as an "incomprehensible" place intensified in some quarters in the wake of the 2010 earthquake, with much coverage of the destruction caused by the cataclysm obscuring the historical and contemporary geopolitical conditions of its possibility.[31]

The continued force of such ideologies, including, as Philogene notes, in the interpretation of "Haitian art," makes Pascale Monnin's call for greater and more in-depth research on the oeuvres of well- and lesser-known Haitian artists seem all the more important. "Everyone talks about Haitian painting as a whole," she notes in her interview with Marcelin, "whereas I think that we have to work to enhance the value of each artist individually to develop Haitian painting in general. It's necessary to document the work of artists. It's necessary to... understand the genealogies of artists, their interconnections" (p. 45). She specifies that this documentation should include, when possible, ongoing oral historical research. In implicitly critiquing the ways in which Haitian painting has been pigeon-holed since the 1940s, Monnin suggests that closer attention to the work and interconnections of differently positioned artists, past and present, has the potential to transform perceptions of the larger field.

How the respective paintings of artists such as Sacha Tebó (cat. nos. 24 and 25), Mario Benjamin (cat. no. 4), and Florine Demosthene (cat. no. 8) defy stereotypical assumptions about "Haitian art" may be immediately recognizable — and, indeed, throughout his career Benjamin has framed his work, in part, as a challenge to the preconceptions attached to that category. However Monnin's comments suggest that greater in-depth research on the artistic development and production of those who have been automatically slotted into the *"naïf* school" would likewise problematize and transform such received understandings. Her call for greater research on "genealogy" is, in fact, particularly significant with regard to the work of such artists insofar as artistic genealogy is precisely what early promoters often occluded in order to guarantee the originality and authenticity of those they called the "primitive painters."

The research for which Monnin calls necessitates rethinking not only the label *"naïf"* (evidently problematic) but also "self-taught," a seemingly more innocuous designation that again discounts genealogy by disregarding family- or community-based processes of artistic development.[32] Certainly such a genealogical project would need to take into consideration, as Célius examines in his essay, the ways in which subaltern artists (among others) have drawn on multiple iconographies, religious and otherwise, for artistic reinterpretation and transfiguration. It might also entail, as Edouard Duval-Carrié has suggested, reconsidering so-called *"naïf"* works produced under the François and Jean-Claude Duvalier dictatorships (1957-1986), featuring as he puts it "[t]hose 'de rigueur' tilled, well-organised fields, and the brightly painted architectural renditions of urban life on canvas," precisely for their seemingly absent political commentary. Disparaged as derivative, generic, tourist productions, such paintings might better be understood, he argues, as "sub-conscious demands on a government that had the utmost contempt for its population and its needs. Hence to think that these were works of art stemming from naïve minds is tantamount to bad faith."[33]

Prioritizing artistic interconnections — both local and transnational — as part of such genealogical work might build on the bodies of research examining links among Haitian, African American, and Cuban painters in the 1930s and 1940s, as well as the significance that André Breton's "discovery" of Hector Hyppolite's work had for the course of both Haitian painting and international surrealism. In the contemporary moment, such research might explore, following Célius's and Philogene's leads, how prominent artists such as Vladimir Cybil Charlier, Ebony G. Patterson, Guyodo (Frantz Jacques), Killy (Patrick Ganthier), Lionel

St.-Eloi, Edouard Duval-Carrié, and Monnin herself have adapted the techniques and idiom of *drapo* creation in their own diverse sculptural and mixed media works — in certain cases collaborating with *drapo* creators.

In short, the contributors to this catalogue and the artists featured in the exhibition advance the project of "re-framing" how Haitian artistic production, in its diversity and complexity, is approached, analyzed, and understood.[34] To explore the artistic genealogies of artists without formal training and to examine how "Haitian art" has long been shaped by and itself shaped international artistic currents, is to break with ideologies that have sustained problematic assumptions about Haitian artistic production, as well as about Haitian history, culture, and society. In spotlighting the stylistic and thematic dialogue of Haitian artists across disciplines, generations, and national boundaries, *Transformative Visions* is mounted in the hope and expectation that these works will enable viewers to see Haitian art — and thus Haiti and the world — in new ways.[35]

***

[1]Annie Paul, "Visualizing Art in the Caribbean," in *Infinite Island: Contemporary Caribbean Art*, ed. Tumelo Mosaka (Brooklyn, NY: Brooklyn Museum in Association with Philip Wilson Publishers, 2008), 30.

[2]On the history of *drapo* see Patrick Polk, "Sacred Banners and the Divine Cavalry Charge," in *Sacred Arts of Haitian Vodou*, ed. Donald J. Cosentino (Los Angeles: UCLA Fowler Museum of Cultural History, 1995), 325-347. On Bazile's work specifically see Anna Wexler, "An Interview with Clotaire Bazile," *Callaloo* 20, no. 2 (1997): 383-398. Many thanks to Anna Wexler for her great role in facilitating the Lowe Art Museum's acquisition of Bazile's *Saint Jacques Majeur* and for discussing his work with me.

[3]Karen McCarthy Brown, "Serving the Spirits: The Ritual Economy of Haitian Vodou," in *Sacred Arts of Haitian Vodou*, ed. Donald J. Cosentino (Los Angeles: UCLA Fowler Museum of Cultural History, 1995), 215.

[4]The United States did not extend diplomatic recognition to Haiti until 1862.

[5]Donald J. Cosentino, "Gede Rising," in *In Extremis: Death and Life in 21st-Century Haitian Art*, ed. Donald J. Cosentino (Los Angeles: Fowler Museum at UCLA, 2012), 27. Early twentieth

century photographs document paintings on the walls of *ounfò* (temples) featuring historical figures identified with particular *lwa* and masonic symbols as well. See for example "Entrance of a Vudu Shrine, Haiti," in *Photos and Phantasms: Harry Johnston's Photographs of the Caribbean* (London: The British Council Royal Geographical Society, 1998), cat. 39.

[6]See Michel-Philippe Lerebours, "The Indigenist Revolt: Haitian Art, 1927-1944," *Callaloo* 15, no. 3 (Summer 1992): 721; Lewis Ampidu Clorméus, "Entre l'État, les élites et les religions en Haïti. Redécouvrir la campagne antisuperstitieuse de 1939-1942," Ph.D. diss., École des Hautes Études en Sciences Sociales/Université d'Etat d'Haïti, 2012; Kate Ramsey, *The Spirits and the Law: Vodou and Power in Haiti* (Chicago: The University of Chicago Press, 2011), 101-117 and 193-210.

[7]See Michel-Philippe Lerebours, "A History of Haitian Painting," trans. Jessica Adams and Cécile Accilien, in *Revolutionary Freedoms: A History of Survival, Strength and Imagination in Haiti*, eds. Cécile Accilien, Jessica Adams, and Elmide Méléance (Coconut Creek, FL: Caribbean Studies Press, 2006), 154-156. See also Gérald Alexis, *Peintres haïtiens/Haitian Painters* (Paris: Éditions Cercle d'Art), 17-26.

[8]Jean Price-Mars, *Ainsi parla l'oncle* (1928; Ottawa: Éditions Leméac, 1973), 255 and 258.

[9]Savain was influenced in his choice of subjects, in part, by the example of African American painter William Edouard Scott who traveled to Haiti in 1931 on a grant from the Julius Rosenwald Fund and produced a large body of work focused on peasant life, labor, and culture. See Krista Thompson, "Preoccupied with Haiti: The Dream of Diaspora in African American Art, 1915-1942," *American Art* 21, no. 3 (Fall 2007): 87; and Michel-Philippe Lerebours, "The Indigenist Revolt: Haitian Art, 1927-1944," *Callaloo* 15, no. 3 (Summer 1992): 714-716.

[10]Katherine Smith, "Haitian Art and the Vodou Imaginary," in *Kafou: Haiti, Art, and Vodou*, eds. Alex Farquharson and Leah Gordon (Nottingham, England: Nottingham Contemporary, 2013), 37.

[11]Leah Gordon, "Kreyon Pèp La Pa Gen Gòm (The People's Pencil has no Eraser)," in *Kafou: Haiti, Art, and Vodou*, eds. Alex Farquharson and Leah Gordon (Nottingham, England: Nottingham Contemporary, 2013), 23.

[12]Karen McCarthy Brown, "Interview with Edouard Duval-Carrié," February 1995, Miami, in *Tracing the Spirit: Ethnographic Essays on Haitian Art* (Davenport, IA: Davenport Museum of Art, 1995), 75.

[13]See Donald J. Cosentino's analysis of this series of paintings in Cosentino, *Divine Revolution: The Art of Edouard Duval-Carrié* (Los Angeles: UCLA Fowler Museum of Cultural History, 2004), 40-47.

[14]Quoted by Donald J. Cosentino in "Lespri Endepandan: Discovering Haitian Sculpture," in *Lespri Endepandan: Discovering Haitian Sculpture*, cur. Elizabeth Cerejido (Miami: The Patricia & Phillip Frost Art Museum, Florida International University, 2004), 9.

[15]As Barbara Prézeau-Stephenson has noted of other Duval-Carrié works, these trees index the royal palm topped with a Phrygian cap that appears as a symbol of freedom on the Haitian flag and is also associated with the *lwa* Ayizan. See Barbara Prézeau-Stephenson, "Contemporary Art as Cultural Product in the Context of Haiti," trans. Rachel Douglas, *Small Axe* 12, no. 3 (October 2008): 98.

16This was transcribed by Gage Averill as sung by Gérard Dupervil. See Averill's *A Day for the Hunter, A Day for the Prey: Popular Music and Power in Haiti* (Chicago: University of Chicago Press, 1997), 67-68. Interestingly, given the connection between Duval-Carrié's *Trois Feuilles* and *Trois Fois Simbie,* Averill notes that the song is "directed to the deity Simbi, a guardian of springs for whom 'Simbi twa fèy' and 'Simbi twa rasin' are two avatars." See also Gerdès Fleurant's discussion of the idea of *twa fèy, twa rasin* in analyzing the significance of the number three more generally in his *Dancing Spirits: Rhythms and Rituals of Haitian Vodun, the Rada Rite* (Westport, CT: Praeger, 1996), 26. See too the interesting discussion of the significance of this song on the parts of Edwidge Danticat, Laurent Dubois, and Elizabeth McAlister among others in the roundtable convened by Sasha Frere-Jones in the online edition of *The New Yorker* on March 24, 2009.

17Préfète Duffaut interviewed by Louis Herns Marcelin, May 12, 2011 in Jacmel, Haiti, and December 15, 2011 in Martissant, Haiti.

18In an interview with Jerry Philogene, artist Vladimir Cybil suggests that Myrlande Constant uses the medium of beads "as paint," and discusses her own "beading" of rice paper. Jerry Philogene, "Vladimir Cybil," *BOMB* 90 (Winter 2005), web.

19Myrlande Constant interviewed by Louis Herns Marcelin, July 15, 2014 in Carrefour-Feuilles, Haiti. See also Gina Athena Ulysse, "Constant: Haiti's Fiercest Flag Bearer," *The Huffington Post* (April 14, 2011), web.

20My thanks to Louis Herns Marcelin for reminding me of this important point.

21Enclosure in letter from Francoise Arnesen, Proprietor, Mapou Galerie, Pétionville, Haiti, to Brian Dursum, Director, Lowe Art Museum, January 9, 2000. Filed in the acquisition folder for this painting at the Lowe Art Museum.

22On the "cyberpunk" sensibilities of this work, see Donald J. Cosentino, "Gede Rising," in *In Extremis: Death and Life in 21st-Century Haitian Art*, ed. Donald J. Cosentino (Los Angeles: Fowler Museum at UCLA, 2012), 57; and Leah Gordon, "Kreyon Pèp La Pa Gen Gòm (The People's Pencil has no Eraser)," in *Kafou: Haiti, Art, Vodou*, eds. Alex Farquharson and Leah Gordon (Nottingham, England: Nottingham Contemporary, 2013), 24. See their respective writings on the work of Grand Rue artists more generally and also Katherine Smith, "Atis Rezistans: Gede and the Art of Vagabondaj," in *Obeah* and *Other Powers: The Politics of Caribbean Religion and Healing*, eds. Diana Paton and Maarit Forde (Durham: Duke University Press, 2012), 121-145.

23Edwidge Danticat, "Lòt Bò Dlo, The Other side of the Water," in Paul Farmer, ed., *Haiti After the Earthquake* (New York: PublicAffairs, 2011), 257.

24J. Michael Dash, "Fictions of Displacement: Locating Modern Haitian Narratives," *Small Axe* 27 (October 2008): 41.

25See Donald J. Cosentino, "Gede Rising," in *In Extremis: Death and Life in 21st-Century Haitian Art*, ed. Donald J. Cosentino (Los Angeles: Fowler Museum at UCLA, 2012), 180, footnote 12.

[26]See Célius's chapter "De l'hégémonie de l'art naïf" (99-190) in his *Langage plastique et énonciation identitaire: L'invention de l'art haïtien* (Québec: Les Presses de l'Université Laval, 2007), especially 146-150.

[27]Quoted in Michel-Philippe Lerebours, "A History of Haitian Painting," trans. Jessica Adams and Cécile Accilien in *Revolutionary Freedoms: A History of Survival, Strength and Imagination in Haiti*, eds. Cécile Accilien, Jessica Adams, and Elmide Méléance (Coconut Creek, FL: Caribbean Studies Press, 2006), 164. For the full text of the manifesto see Célius, *Langage plastique et énonciation identitaire: L'invention de l'art haïtien* (Québec: Les Presses de l'Université Laval, 2007), 199.

[28]Carlo Célius, *Langage plastique et énonciation identitaire: L'invention de l'art haïtien* (Québec: Université Laval, 2007), 164-165.

[29]W. B. Seabrook, *The Magic Island* (New York: Harcourt, Brace and Company, 1929).

[30]Michel-Rolph Trouillot, "The Odd and the Ordinary: Haiti, the Caribbean, and the World," *Cimarrón: New Perspectives on the Caribbean* 2, no. 3 (Winter 1990): 7 and 11.

[31]See Sibylle Fischer, "Beyond Comprehension," *Social Text*, Periscope: "Ayiti Kraze/Haiti in Fragments," web. Also see J. Michael Dash, "Haiti: Seismic Shock or Paradigm Shift," *Social Text*, Periscope: "Ayiti Kraze/Haiti in Fragments," web; and Nadège T. Clitandre, "Haitian Exceptionalism in the Caribbean and the Project of Rebuilding Haiti," *Journal of Haitian Studies* 17, no. 2 (Fall 2011): 146-153.

[32]See Alex Farquharson's discussion of such labels in his catalogue essay for *Kafou: Haiti, Art, Vodou:* "'Self-taught'…is only factually correct from the perspective of a narrow, elitist definition of art pedagogy. Few artists in *Kafou* worked or work in isolation: most learnt from the examples of others, belong to collectives, received formal training, or produced their work in conscious dialogue with historical or contemporary developments in the larger art world. For the same reasons, in a densely populated country whose culture is highly familial, social and collective, the label 'outsider', with its connotations of extreme isolation, applies to very few Haitian artists." Alex Farquharson, "Kafou — At the Crossroads," in *Kafou: Haiti, Art and Vodou*, eds. Alex Farquharson and Leah Gordon (Nottingham, England: Nottingham Contemporary, 2013), 10.

[33]Edouard Duval-Carrié in *Kafou: Haiti, Art and Vodou*, eds. Alex Farquharson and Leah Gordon (Nottingham, England: Nottingham Contemporary, 2013), 206-207.

[34]This references "Re-Framing Haiti: Art, History and Performativity," a multi-venue collaboration by Brown University, the Rhode Island School of Design, and the Waterloo Center for the Arts, directed by Anthony Bogues, Katherine Smith, and Karen Allen Baxter.

[35]I am grateful to Louis Herns Marcelin and Tim Watson for their invaluable input and feedback on this essay.

CONVERSATION WITH PASCALE MONNIN

Louis Herns Marcelin

LOUIS HERNS MARCELIN: HOW DID YOUR PATH AS AN ARTIST BEGIN, FROM SWITZERLAND TO HAITI AND FROM HAITI TO THE WORLD?

PASCALE MONNIN: My grandfather came to Haiti to live in the 1940s. My father was brought up here [in Haiti]. That's how I was born in Port-au-Prince. I went back to Switzerland at the age of 3 after my parents divorced, but I never lost my connection with Haiti.

The back-and-forth shaped me and I claim a multiple, complex, and paradoxical identity.

My grandfather, Roger Monnin, opened the Galerie Monnin in 1956. Thus from an early age, I met lots of Haitian artists, and I visited galleries with my father. As far back as I can remember, there were always paintings, artists, and art lovers at the house.

L.H.M.: SO YOU GREW UP IN THE ART ENVIRONMENT?

P.M.: Completely! Both here in Haiti and in Switzerland. My mother was a professor of manual arts: she taught woodworking and ironworking and bookbinding. Reading and painting were also popular at home. When I was a child, she always provided some kind of materials and objects for me to tinker with. She taught me lots of techniques. Very young, without ever attending art school, I knew how to do lots of things. We made carnival masks, did bookbinding, collage, needlework. Since my earliest childhood, I was immersed in an artistic milieu with artists, but also in a very manual environment where we made lots of things. For me, this was always evidence that I too was an artist.

I first followed a literary curriculum — Latin, English — all the while keeping up with design classes at the academy. I then discovered that the County of Geneva was attempting an innovative experiment: that is how my registration was accepted and I was able to prepare and obtain an artistic baccalaureate from the Voltaire College of Geneva.

This particular training turned out to be exhilarating; this is how I was able to learn to engrave on copper and to participate in sculpture, ceramics, design, and painting workshops.

All that between the age of 15 and 19, which are the formative years! And what's more, it answered all my curiosities!

The usual path would have been to study at Beaux-Arts but I was a bit afraid of schools because I saw that contemporary art required a person to *talk* art, whereas I wanted to learn how to *do* art. I decided to start "slogging away"; I did theater scenery, frescoes....

L.H.M.: DURING THAT PERIOD, WHAT MATERIALS DID YOU WORK WITH?

P.M.: I used wood, cardboard, *papier mâché*. I have always loved salvaged materials. I recall making frescoes using fluorescent paint; I made people in *papier mâché*, masks for masquerade parties....

L.H.M.: ALREADY MASKS – WHERE DID THEY COME FROM?

P.M.: An important event that shaped my childhood was the death of my older brother. When I was three years old, my brother was seven. He was a little boy who told his grandmother, "I have a headache," and he went into a coma and died one week later. That's when things changed because my mother decided to leave Haiti and to take me with her.

So I returned to Switzerland and was raised by a mother who had lost her little boy. You could say I had a childhood that was both happy and sad. I remember as a child having a lot of anguish, nightmares. I was a worried child. We used to make plaster masks during carnival time. My mother always had a special relationship to carnival because that's the time of the year when my brother died. Carnival is in essence a bit morbid; it's a time one can do anything one wants as long as one is masked. And so, I began to make casts, masks. But the casting is also related to mortuary masks. I was always fascinated by these imprints. My encounter with plaster occurred by way of carnival and I must have been 13 or 14 years old. For the carnival in the city, I remember having made a series referring to Egyptian gods, of masks with a system of batteries and lights to make them glow at night. One year, I remember making animals. Later, it was the Moscow circus. It was a lot of fun. We were a group of buddies and we wore disguises to the four corners of the city where they still burn the "Old Man Winter" symbolically every year. I won first prize at the Carnival of Yverdon-les-Bains — a city near Lausanne in Switzerland — several years in a row at the end of the 1980s.

L.H.M.: IN ADDITION TO MASKS, HAVE YOU ALSO CULTIVATED OTHER ARTISTIC FORMS USING OTHER MEDIA?

P.M.: Casts are one love among other passions. I drew a lot; I adored and adore to this day engraving. I have always painted a lot. I also did sculpture with a man named Ljuba Stoyanovic, of Serbian origin, who worked in stone and jewels made of melted wax.

I wanted to learn art in the old way — that is, by spending time in workshops, apprenticeship of techniques, crafts. Study art from the artisan side. I also frequented workshops at La Maison Rouge where Pierre Moor taught very classical courses. He began by chromatic color circles. To be able to design from models, a person has to have designed the skeleton, to understand structure before drawing the flesh.

Copper engraving and litho are techniques I adore. Machines in workshops. The odor of acids, lacquers, ink….

L.H.M.: AND WHEN DID YOU BEGIN TO MAKE MOBILES?

P.M.: I remember that during my childhood, in the kitchen, my mother had hung a string to the ceiling to suspend a balance. It was a game: each of us would bring objects and have fun hanging them, all the while re-equilibrating the balance. Little by little this mobile became so large that it took over the entire room.

L.H.M.: AND WHAT AGE WERE YOU AT THAT TIME?

P.M.: I want to say that it was during my adolescence — I can't say exactly. I remember this mobile but there is no photograph to document it. I also remember that finally it was dismantled because it took up too much room....

L.H.M.: AT WHAT TIME DID YOU DECIDE TO RETURN TO HAITI TO LIVE AND HOW DID THIS MOVE AFFECT YOUR ARTISTIC TRAJECTORY?

P.M.: I used to come to Haiti every year on vacation. But at the age of 20, I decided to stay for good. I wanted to give my father a hand, and then, like a thread in the needle, I began to go to the Galerie Monnin — the family gallery. In the course of the same year, I decided to do my first painting exhibit. At the age of 20, I exhibited about 70 to 80 canvases, designs, in all formats, and I sold 90% of the exhibited canvases! Unfortunately, not all later exhibits worked like that!

I have painted a lot and engraved without abandoning the three-dimensional work. I have met artists, friends, visited workshops, done collaborations. I have worked on four-hand paintings with Frantz Zéphirin and organized academic design courses with Sergine André. I have also met Lissa Jeannot, a magnificent ceramist, a Haitian artist who accompanied me for my first series of heads. From there, from this collaboration was born my first exhibition of mobiles. I have cast the faces of friends, children, people I know, and strangers. This first series of masks was exhibited in Haiti in 2006 and later for the *Roots and More* exhibition in 2009 at the Afrika Museum at Berg en Dal, in Holland.

L.H.M.: AND THE MASKS RETURN!

P.M.: Yes, the masks return! Lissa taught me to do raku. Raku is a really interesting Japanese technique with three firings. First you make the cast. Then you make an impression with clay that will be fired once. On this mask, you put the glaze, the raku. Fire it again. This time when you open the kiln, and you take the burning mask out with iron tongs, you plunge it in water. Hot/cold. This causes the cracking that is typical of a successful raku. In the last step, you burn wood shavings in oil drums and in there, the mask is smothered in smoke and soot that infiltrates into the cracks, giving the clay a beautiful color of smoky black. That's raku.

L.H.M.: HOW DO YOU INCORPORATE RAKU INTO YOUR WORK?

P.M.: What's interesting about raku is that you cannot control it. The shapes of the cracks are unpredictable. But as the saying goes, chance is the shadow of God. The fissure, the fault, is interesting, complex. When I cast people, my goal is not necessarily to make a portrait that resembles the person. My intention is to question faces, imprints, and to search in the series to sense the humanity. A cracked raku face appears like a parchment, a labyrinth, scars.

My first exhibit of mobiles is called *My 100 Heads*. It's a play on words [*translator's note*: in French, 100 is *cent*, pronounced similarly to *sans*, meaning "without"] between numbers and forgetfulness, not having a head. The masks may be morbid and very quickly I knew I wanted to show them standing, moving, mobile. I cast living people and I present them as such.

Installation for the *Roots
and More* exhibition, Afrika
Museum, 2009.
© Pascale Monnin

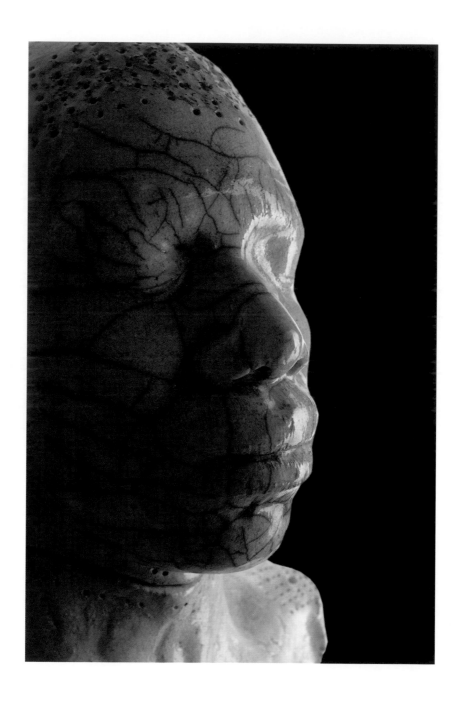

Antoine, 2005.
© Pascale Monnin

L.H.M.: AND YOU PROGRESSIVELY TRANSFORM THEM?

P.M.: In my studio, pieces hang, wait.... I always work on several pieces at the same time. In general, I don't have any idea of the finality of a piece as I work on it. I don't know what it will look like finished.

It evolves little by little. These pieces take shape over years, changing according to the installation, adapting to the location.... My mobiles are a more intimate work than my painting. I don't have any special desire to sell to particular people. I see them instead exhibited in public places....

L.H.M.: DOES THAT HAVE A CONNECTION TO THIS IDEA OF THE EVOLUTION OF THE PIECE? THAT IS, THAT THERE IS NOT A FINAL DETACHMENT?

P.M.: When I sell my paintings, I'm happy that they are leaving. Once I'm done painting them, they are finished. They can go live their life as a painting.

But when I see my heads, my mobiles, I see them as part of a whole, part of a larger series. Perhaps also because they are imprints of people I love, I have difficulty letting them go. The final product is, in my mind, a large exhibition that pulls together all my mobiles. This acquisition at the Lowe Art Museum sheds a new light on it.[1] This mobile takes on the status of finished. Since it's no longer in my studio where I can retouch it, it's finished. Even though it may travel again for another exhibition and I can present it differently....

L.H.M: *L'ANGE DE LA RÉSURRECTION* [CAT. NO. 20] — TELL ME ITS STORY.

P.M.: Originally, its name was not *L'Ange de la Résurrection*; I called it *Antoine*. Just because Antoine was the name of the little boy I cast. He was between 10 and 12 years old. To cast is to fix an instant in the life of someone, and this face, his youth, touched me enormously. His head

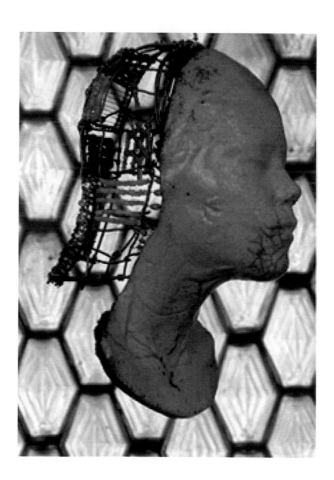

Antoine before and after the break. On the right, as he was exhibited at the Château du Chatelard in Switzerland in 2005 and on the far right, in Pascale Monnin's studio in 2010. © Pascale Monnin.

is very classical, symmetrical, asexual. He has innocence, sweetness, a form of perfection that touches me deeply. His face questions me and I question him. When you cast someone, there is an astonishing phenomenon: when the mask is finished and you look at the face, sometimes you hardly recognize the person who you knew rather well. A face captured in a single expression resembles the person but the reality of someone is also in movement, expressions. The body is obviously not what the person does. When the person settles in for casting, he closes his eyes and does not move. And this is what will be immortalized, trapped. The person that you know then disappears to make room for this other that will become a mythic character, an apparition. For a long time I called him Antoine, up until the moment when I no longer called him by his name. Antoine had given up his place to this angel... this angel who evidently resembles him but is not him.

L.H.M.: AT WHAT MOMENT DID YOU CALL HIM *L'ANGE DE LA RÉSURRECTION?*

P.M.: Oh, that came later! But before he took on that name, there are still more stories because in the beginning *Antoine* had the face of a

L'Ange de la Résurrection in Chelsea, in 2014. © Pascale Monnin

perfect child. He had the raku cracks but he did not yet have the scar that cuts right across his face. What is the scar? One day, during an exhibition in Switzerland, he fell and broke! Oh, dear! I was really very annoyed. I wondered how I was going to glue him back together in a way that wouldn't be seen. And then all of a sudden — and this is something that was going to become a trademark of my work as a result — I said to myself: "But it's not necessary to glue him back together, nor to try to hide it…! Quite the opposite! I have to put him back together and I have to show it! I have to use this for this piece." And that's why I made this scar with diamonds. I did not know if it was going to be a finished piece, like part of my creation is to put together chance occurrences. A piece is designed little by little. The problem gave me new impetus. You have to wear scars as jewels; it's almost philosophical. This piece becomes the symbol of something larger than the portrait of a single individual.

L.H.M.: HE HAD LEFT THE SPACE OF INNOCENCE, THE SPACE OF INDIVIDUALITY. *ANTOINE* WAS IN THE PROCESS OF BECOMING THIS OTHER THING AND HE WAS BEGINNING TO TALK TO YOU….

P.M.: When you meet people, their scars, their features, their wrinkles talk about their life, their path, their age…. In the same way the evolution of my mobiles takes account of the time that passes.

The piece talks about memory, time passing and breaking, and that it's necessary to accept. You have to live with scars. We have to wear them as jewels. Not because we want to but because it's our destiny as mortals on earth.

Antoine became *L'Ange de la Résurrection* in 2011, the year after the earthquake, for an exhibit in New York. I had just finished the body, the wings of another piece, *L'Ange Sacrifié* [Sacrificed Angel] for an exhibit at Agnès B in Paris.

L'Ange Sacrifié is a nod to the book by Alejo Carpentier, *Kingdom of this World.* The book presents the story of Noël, a slave who participates in the Haitian Revolution and is liberated, but ends up a slave to King Christophe. Noël's dream of liberty was sacrificed on the altar of Christophe's power — Christophe who is nevertheless one of the heroes of the Haitian Revolution.[2]

In this installation, four large panels on the walls covered with posters of presidential elections of 2006 and 2010 are the background canvas behind the rotating *L'Ange Sacrifié.*

It is they, the politicians, who sacrifice the individual, just like Noël's dreams were sacrificed by Christophe. This *Angel* is a person with a double face; on one side a man and on the other side a non-face framed by a human jaw. Political engagement is often betrayed by the very ones who dreamed of it and the revolution growls anew. As Bertolt Brecht said, "We have to change the changed world."

L'Ange de la Résurrection was also exhibited at the Rogue Studio in Chelsea, New York. The installation was filmed and set to music by Federico Chieli. My sister later exhibited it at the OAS museum [the Art Museum of the Americas of the Organization of American States] in Washington. *L'Ange de la Résurrection* is a matching piece to *L'Ange Sacrifié.*

As you see, the face of *L'Ange de la Résurrection* has a raku that is less cracked than that of *L'Ange Sacrifié.* His face is much softer. It's also the child's rather than the man's face. On the cheek, there is a little green, and this green comes from the fact that in the kiln the piece was not far from another piece that had a copper glaze and simply the proximity to the other colored Antoine's cheek. Chance or decision? You have to be reborn to continue, life is change, the wings of this angel also make you think of the chrysalis that means a change in form.

L'Ange Sacrifié, 2011.
© Pascale Monnin.

L.H.M.: *L'ANGE DE LA RÉSURRECTION* AND *L'ANGE SACRIFIÉ* ARE PART OF A SERIES?

P.M.: Of course, these two pieces are part of the series *My 100 Heads*, which are less and less "heads" now that they begin to have bodies; these faces of friends, of passers-by that I have cast and that live in my studio.

And then there is another sub-series: the winged mobiles…. A blue angel is now added to two white angels, *Eustache or the Elegy of Complexity*.

L.H.M.: YOU DON'T HAVE IT HERE IN YOUR STUDIO?

P.M.: No, no, it is now in the Château of Val Fleury in Gif-sur-Yvette, in France, from September 11 until October 24, 2014. It was also exhibited in April 2014 at the Manoir de Martigny in Switzerland.

And finally it will be shown at the Grand Palais in Paris at the end of this year.

We must also talk about the presentation of these pieces. Shadows and light are fundamental. My mobiles need a luminous staging. The pieces have a life with multiple facets depending on the lighting and the place.

The shadows are a work in themselves. Sometimes the shadows seem more alive than the pieces. *L'Ange de la Résurrection* was presented in New York not long ago and I really liked that the *Angel* had two shadows with two beams of light.

L.H.M.: HOW ARE THESE LIGHTS ORGANIZED?

P.M.: There is no law. It is a function of the places, the space available, the natural lighting or not. This is the reason I generally travel to install my pieces. I like to be there. I would love to be able to work with a lighting artist; somebody I don't know yet but who would be able to give me some ideas. I enjoy continuing to work on this aspect of my installations. My pieces are hung from a little motor that makes them rotate, that creates movement. The shadow created becomes as alive, even more alive than the piece itself. *Eustache* at the Grand Palais will have a new staging: a canvas tent. If one approaches from the back, one will be able to see only the shadow but from the other side, the tent will be open and the visitor will also be able to see the piece itself.

L.H.M.: EVEN WHEN A PIECE IS ACQUIRED, IT IS STILL LIVING; IT CAN BE WORKED, REWORKED, REINVENTED THROUGH SHADOWS AND LIGHTING.

P.M.: Perfectly! I always insist on being there for the mounting of my mobiles. It's very important for me to be there to mount *L'Ange de la Résurrection* at the Lowe Art Museum in November. There is a type of re-creation of the work through the re-positioning and the lighting. All my pieces can also be disassembled. You can remove the wings, and take off the head. The *Angel* goes home in a suitcase.

L.H.M.: HOW DO YOU SEE THE RELATIONSHIP BETWEEN *L'ANGE DE LA RÉSURRECTION*, *L'ANGE SACRIFIÉ*, AND *EUSTACHE OR THE ELEGY OF COMPLEXITY*? ARE THEY COMPLEMENTARY?

P.M.: These pieces explore different facets of the human condition. These angels tend toward something on the order of the universal. *L'Ange Sacrifié*, *L'Ange de la Résurrection*, and *Eustache or the Elegy of Complexity* are on the order of the mythic.

L.H.M.: TELL ME A BIT MORE ABOUT *EUSTACHE*...

P.M.: The history of this piece begins with James Noël, my husband, who, when we were in New Caledonia, came back from a trip with a gift made to order for me. Rather than bringing me flowers, he brought the skull of a stag, and it is one of the most beautiful gifts I have ever received [laughter].

Eustache in its second form in a sort of cave at the
Villa Medici in Rome in 2013. © Pascale Monnin

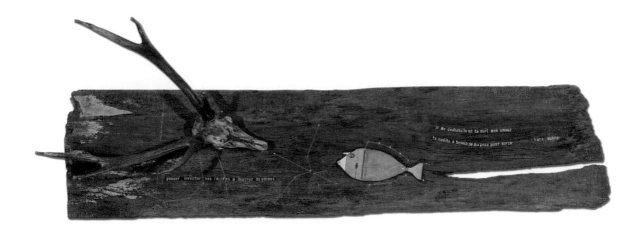

The Stag and the Dawa, 50 x 300 cm. © Pascale Monnin

The first time I exhibited this head, it was not yet a mobile, but an installation.

I had put the stag face forward on the wood and I had put him in discussion with a *Dawa*, a fish that is endemic to New Caledonia. The encounter of the two animals was the subject of a pertinent observation by an indigenous man on the evening of the private viewing. He saw in this face-to-face an encounter between the West — the stag imported by the French colonists — and the indigenous Kanaks — [represented by] the *Dawa*, which is one of the totem animals of Kanak culture.

Stags are not endemic to New Caledonia. French colonists imported them and let them loose into the wild. They have reproduced so much that today stags have destabilized the environmental equilibrium of the fauna on the island. To the point that today, if you kill a stag and you bring his head to City Hall, they will pay you. Without knowing this history, I had put a little iron Christ between the stag's horns.

Later, in Rome, the stag became *Eustache* when I discovered a church with this name. *Eustache* is a saint of the New Testament. A hunter finds himself in the middle of the forest face to face with a stag. He aims at him. Suddenly, in the middle of the stag's horns, an apparition of Christ holds back his hand and he is converted.

The stag symbolizes for me the conquering Catholicism, colonialism, but this head is doubled with the face of a child. Faith is also pure when it is lived individually.

Later I put the face of a child in a mirror in place of *Eustache*, reversible, and at this moment the name changed....

For the installation at the Grand Palais, it will be called *Eustache or the Elegy of Complexity.*

L.H.M.: WHEN YOU LOOK AT THE ARTISTIC LANDSCAPE IN HAITI, WHAT HAS CHANGED? WHAT CAN YOU TELL US ABOUT NEW SCHOOLS OF ARTISTS IN HAITI COMPARED TO 20 TO 30 YEARS AGO?

P.M.: I would say that art in Haiti is very alive today but it has changed profoundly in recent years. The political and economic situation of the country has also influenced the course of events. There is the question of the market. Two currents have appeared: yesterday, it was the Grands Naïfs, the Saint-Soleils, the Naïfs Précieux, the Ecole de la Beauté. Today, there are the Contemporains, the Artists of Grand Rue, the Artists of Bel Air, and artists evolving outside of Haiti, in the Caribbean, Canada, the United States, Africa, and in Europe.

We missed the opportunity to develop the popularity of artists on the international level. The ongoing political and economic crises that affect this country, the natural disasters that bring the curious or humanitarian workers have not helped us do the basic work of developing our patrimony. There is an institutional void in regulating and protecting various agents. Problems of forgeries, lack of experts, art historians, university people writing their dissertations, art schools with chronic problems of being accessible and open to the world, are some of the factors that do not promote the diffusion and enhancement of our present and past artistic production.

In spite of all the problems exposed, the artistic scene remains very fertile and interesting. Bridges are being built between authors and painters.

You have seen the work that we are doing with James, my husband, with the literary journal *IntranQu'illités*,[3] which is heading down this path. The twenty-first century has its failings but also its advantages. Today, thanks to the Internet, a person can produce a review in Port-au-Prince and solicit artists, writers, and photographers from around the world. Pierre Soulages — the French father of *outrenoir* — did the cover of the third issue of our journal and stands beside Georges Liautaud — iconic Haitian artist of the 1960s — or Josué Azor — a young photographer. Dany Laferrière, our Haitian academician, rubs shoulders with Paul Harry Laurent — unknown poet — or Marie Darrieussecq — French writer — or Jorge Luis Borges — Argentinian author.

L.H.M.: CAN YOU TELL ME ABOUT THE HAITIAN SOCIAL ELITE AND THEIR ROLE IN PROMOTING HAITIAN ART? IS THERE A NATIONAL MARKET — FOR EXAMPLE PRIVATE INSTITUTIONS, BANKS, ETC. DO THEY COLLECT?

P.M.: That's an interesting question! Haitian painting is hardly collected by Haitians themselves. Evidently some individuals have beautiful collections, and that's a good thing, but it is not common. My father at one time tried to meet influential people in banks to say, "You should build collections; art can also be an excellent investment; an artist who becomes famous can have a great return. It is important to put together a collection for the future of your institution." The response shows the gap a bit, the lack of comprehension of the market for art in an international context: "Ah, if you like, you can exhibit your paintings in our branches." There is no policy for developing our cultural patrimony.

Haitian art is perhaps more famous outside the country than in Haiti itself. Just look at how many museums we have. We had two and the earthquake destroyed one.

Everyone talks about Haitian painting as a whole, whereas I think that we have to work to enhance the value of each artist individually to develop Haitian painting in general. It's necessary to document the work of artists. It's necessary to do what you of the University of Miami in Florida and the Institut Interuniversitaire de Recherche et Développement (INURED) in Haiti are doing with me: understand the genealogies of artists, their interconnections. There are exhibition catalogues but not many monographs. Some artists who are icons don't have monographs, even less a catalogue. Deceased artists like Philomé Obin, Gabriel Liautaud, and Préfète Duffaut don't have monographs even though they are considered major artists. This is not an isolated case; this is the case of the majority of great Haitian artists. I think you can count on the fingers of one hand the number of artists who have monographs. Mario Benjamin, Hector Hyppolite, Tiga. It seems that only recently people have begun to become conscious of these problems but we have to get to work seriously and systematically. We must understand that culture is a wealth in peril that needs to be developed.

I just finished a monograph on an artist named Gérard Fortuné. I chose him because he is one of the oldest "naïve" artists and I find his work and the man himself enchanting. I thought I knew his work but in doing research I discovered thousands of things.

A small anecdote: he painted a painting in which you see a lady walking a dog at the end of a leash. For me it was the lady with the dog, period! After that, I thought about it: here in Haiti, do you often see ladies walking with dogs? Never! I asked Gérard what this painting represents and he calmly explained to me that the dog is not a dog but a *mandinga* spirit and the woman is an initiate.

It is fundamental and immensely interesting to ask artists about their own works.

Today it is very difficult to find information on artists. So in my spare time, I started to add information to *Wikipedia*. And I realized to what extent reliable and verifiable information was lacking. We don't know much about our artists even though they are considered icons. There is enormous work to be done. We could have students and researchers simply put down on paper what we already know to then give someone else a desire to continue this research....

As I told you at the beginning of this interview, I had the chance to bathe in the artistic Haitian environment and I sincerely admire what has been done and what is being done.

There is also another reality regarding Haitian painting that complicates the research, and that is that 70 to 80% of the Haitian patrimony is not or is no longer in Haiti. The pieces are in Europe, the United States, or Canada! It is thus very difficult to work on this patrimony, but luckily with new technology such as the Internet, it is possible to glean information everywhere. On the other hand, it would require creating a center, a digital platform that pulls together this information and makes it possible to diffuse it and make it accessible.

This is what Haitian universities should do. The university, like everyone, talks about Haitian culture, Haitian art; but what is being done on an institutional level for culture, for art? Nothing!

There were two museums before the earthquake, and now there is only one! In the same way that you were telling me that the INURED report on universities argues that universities were destroyed well before the earthquake, the same goes for the artistic environment and its institutions in Haiti.

The way to promote art in Haiti is not only by creating a national art school; it also involves the development of studios. And improved prestige for works of art. How do we transmit the knowledge and techniques? This takes place in artists' studios. An artist often has students, people who work with him or her when he/she has an order. It is also these same students who will sometimes become forgers, but that's another story....

Finally, there is an enormous task of archiving, cataloguing, authentication, and memory to do. If we wanted to document painting from the 1950s until today, to preserve the memory, it needs to be done now because the witnesses are still here to inform us, but if we miss the boat, this information will be lost forever. In Haiti there is a problem of preservation, of memory.

L.H.M.: BUT THE GALLERIES DO A MINIMUM OF CONSERVATION, DON'T THEY? IT WOULD BE A WORK OF COLLECTION AND SHARING OF CATALOGUED DATA? CENTRALIZATION FOR THE DIFFUSION OF INFORMATION?

P.M.: Yes. I think that is fundamental. This centralization effort can only be done through an institution with an international scope. For example, I have all the files from the Galerie Monnin since 1956. I have saved all the papers, sales books, etc. I have boxes of paperwork where they have recorded what painting was sold to whom. This information could be used to research a painting, to make publishable catalogues. It's necessary to ask other galleries to open their files to students. Le Centre d'Art, La Galerie Saieh, Le Musée d'Art, Les Galeries Nader could constitute a base to start with. It would require creating a sort of *Wikipedia* of Haitian culture. When I see people who want to do dissertations and the problems they have finding information, I see the necessity of collecting this information and making it accessible. Another example: most writing on Haitian painting is in catalogues of exhibitions that were printed in quantities of 500 to 1,000 copies that will never be reprinted. These catalogues could be scanned and put online. I think that if we contact the authors or the institutions that produced these catalogues and ask them, "Can we digitize your catalogues and make them available online for research and cultural development?" I am sure that the majority would say yes, because they know that there is no cost for reprinting and that in this way their work will have a second life. This makes it possible to put together a collection of digital documents that can be used online by people around the world who study and are interested in Haitian art.

L.H.M.: WHO ARE THE HAITIAN ARTISTS WHO HAVE TOUCHED YOU THE MOST? WHO INFORMED YOU THE MOST?

P.M.: That's a question that's very difficult for me to answer because my tastes are diverse and multiple. I'll begin with the artists of the "first generation" who I find fascinating: Hector Hyppolite, Philomé Obin, and Rigaud Benoit. Then there are the portraitists of Vodou such as Gérard Paul, André Pierre, and Camy Rocher. There are also unknown artists, those who made the Vodou flags and religious objects but did not sign them. They are absolutely sublime. I love Georges Liautaud, Pierre-Joseph Valcin, Louisiane Saint Fleurent, and the Saint-Soleil. And then Manès Descollines, Carlo Jean-Jacques in the 1970s to the 1980s. More recently Mario Benjamin, Patrick Vilaire, Maksaens Denis, Ulrick Désert, and I could go on....

Another thing that pleases me a lot here in Haiti is the eruption of art in incongruous places. In the streets of the city, on the collective buses, on the walls of hair salons, in the Vodou temples etc. Here art lives — not just in museums and galleries.

L.H.M.: DO YOU SEE A PRE- AND POST-EARTHQUAKE DIFFERENCE IN CONTEMPORARY HAITIAN ART? WAS THE EARTHQUAKE A MARKER MOMENT IN THE ARTISTIC LANDSCAPE OF HAITI, IN THE DESTRUCTION OF THE EFFORTS THAT MINIMALLY SUPPORTED PAINTING, THE VISIBILITY OF ARTISTS?

P.M.: The cultural environment was already rather unbalanced before the earthquake. Haiti is not at its first end of the world. For a long time now, people in foreign countries have only talked about Haiti when there are political problems or natural disasters such as hurricanes or the earthquake. These are the only times when the world thinks about Haiti. This is when the journalists and humanitarians come, and while they're at it, before leaving again, visit the galleries! So sometimes galleries do better business during crises! This is because there is no more tourism and Haitians do not value painting or other Haitian art forms. It's also a consequence of the lack of vision of successive governments that have not developed the positive aspects of the country.

Since the 1980s Haitian painting has been used too often to find money for charitable work. I don't think this has been good in commercial terms or in terms of recognition. A certain type of Haitian art has moved toward "painting by the meter": repetitive painting that is more a matter of artisanship and for which prices are low, but that is presented without discernment under the label of Haitian painting. And that caused a downward leveling. I would say that the earthquake broke something that was already falling apart.

L.H.M.: AND WOMEN? WOMEN ARTISTS?

P.M.: That's the big question! Women have a minority presence in art. It's as if the art profession is reserved for men. Most women who paint are of privileged social origins or come from educated environments. In the popular classes, girls rarely paint. We are in a society that is rather patriarchal even if in reality the mother is often central and dominant in the family organization. In the cultural sector, one will find more women in the artisanal sector than in the art environment. One major exception is Louisiane Saint Fleurant of the Saint-Soleil movement and today her daughter Magda Magloire.... But when you look in detail how she arrived in Saint-Soleil, it is rather edifying. She was the cook for Tiga, the founder and inspiration of this group, and he had the intelligence to recognize her talent! Almost all the others were men.

There is also a movement called "Les Dames de la Tête de l'Eau [Ladies of the Head of Water]" that gathered together women of good society who drew and painted: Luce Turnier, Tamara Baussan, Michèle Manuel….

However, there are more Haitian women artists here today and a large number are evolving elsewhere in the diaspora. Here in Haiti, there are Tessa Mars, Barbara Prézeau; in the United States, Vladimir Cybil Charlier; in Canada, Marie-Hélène Cauvin; in France, Élodie Barthélémy. I just recently discovered Gaëlle Choisne who I find interesting….There are women artists, but there is no parity, far from it. It would be interesting, for example, to see what goes on in art schools and cinema schools today. Are many girls enrolled, for example?

L.H.M.: FOR SOMEONE COMING OUT OF THE LOWE ART MUSEUM, AFTER VISITING YOUR PIECE, WHAT WOULD YOU LIKE THEM TO TAKE AWAY?

A questioning, a dream…. As you have read, my piece has a history, or rather several stories, but I don't think they are the only possible ones…. A person recognizes or does not recognize herself or himself in a work as a function of what they have lived, their references. If a few see or feel something while looking at my piece, it has been worth the journey.

Laboule, Haiti
June 22, 2014

***

[1] In reference to the acquisition of *L'Ange de la Résurrection* by the Lowe Art Museum.

[2] Alejo Carpentier *Le Royaume de ce monde (El Reino de este mundo)*. Paris: Gallimard, 1954.

[3] *IntranQu'illités* literary and artistic journal created by James Noël and Pascale Monnin in 2012.

METAMORPHOSES

Carlo A. Célius

The world of Haitian visual art is diverse and dynamic.[1] Several driving forces explain the changes that have taken place since the 1930s. Two of these are fundamental: the irruption of the subalterns and the concomitant opening of imaginaries of *oraliture*.[2] Three aspects of the artistic practices that developed in the intervening decades will be analyzed here: the use of available iconographic references, the emergent modes of expression, and the investment and reinvestment in particular techniques and materials.

IRRUPTION OF THE SUBALTERNS

During the nineteenth century (Haiti gained its independence in 1804) the elites valued just one creative field: the fine arts, inherited from the colonial period. A renewal occurred between the 1930s and 1950s. The essential event was the irruption in two phases of the subaltern into the realm of fine arts. The pictorial movement of the 1930s broadened the range of themes that could be addressed. Portraits and historical subjects lost their former preeminence and there was a growing preference for subjects from peasant and urban working class communities. Even in a folklorized mode, this was a transgression in the field of fine arts, which up to that point had been a symbolic space for the self-representation of the elites, fulfilling a purpose of social differentiation. Beginning in the 1940s, the boundary crossings were no longer simply a matter of thematic enlargement. In the new artistic current that was taking over, the subaltern was not only a source of themes with which to work. Rather they — both men and women of this class — became creators themselves. In a social model based on the exclusion and "barbarization" of the "masses," such an event was bound to shake up established social values. The major phenomenon of twentieth-century artistic life in Haiti was that those marginalized began to *speak out both individually and collectively.*

This irruption of the subaltern led to a reconfiguration of the country's visual arts entailing the subversion of the fine arts by the imposition of an unexpected kind of figurative representation, which the establishment immediately rejected; a widening of the social base of the fine arts; the development of divergent trends; the growing visibility of other creative fields, notably the arts of Vodou; the establishment of new relationships between the various fields; the emergence of new dynamics in the circulation of forms, themes, motifs, signs, symbols, and stylistic proposals in the fine arts; and the reorganization of the art marketplace.

Since the 1980s and 1990s, we have witnessed the emergence of different types of creation that distinguish themselves from established trends. These include sculptures in stone and wood, or made from found objects. Artists have been exploring practices such as installation, performance, video art, and photography. These same artists, and others, have also endeavored to bring a new form of painting to life. Artists born in or working in the diaspora have come to the fore, introducing new problematics while, for the most part, remaining in synergy with creators in Haiti. A *new artistic scene* is asserting itself, represented in the Lowe Art Museum's collection with works by Edouard Duval-Carrié (cat. no. 10), André Eugène (cat. no. 11), Mario Benjamin (cat. no. 4), Myrlande Constant (cat. no. 7), Pascale Monnin (cat. no. 20), and Florine Demosthene (cat. no. 8).

This new scene is not the result of a mere generational change. It is not a "school" or a trend. It is spatially spread out and includes artists with diverse careers and a range of artistic projects. However, it is also the extension of an earlier internal process that gives increased visibility to different creative fields, to their interaction, and to transformations in which subalterns continue to play a significant and central role. Several of the creators come from modest social backgrounds, and several centers of creativity have asserted themselves at the heart of the movement. They emerged in peripheral towns and poor neighborhoods of the metropolitan area and include Grand Rue, Bel Air, Rivière Froide, and Carrefour-Feuilles.

AN ICONOGRAPHIC RESOURCE

A social dynamic has marked the world of visual arts creation in Haiti since the first half of the twentieth century. It is both a constant and a source of renewal. It is also connected to another visible line of continuity: the consistent use of certain iconographic references as a resource available for transfiguration and transformation.

The iconographic references are provided by Catholic imagery. They can be seen in the *Troisième tentation* by Préfète Duffaut (cat. no. 9), in Gabriel Lévêque's *Five Angels with Musical Instruments* (cat. no. 17), and in Alexandre Grégoire's *Madonna and Child with Altars to Lwa* (cat. no. 13). They are present under the names Ezili and Saint Jacques in Clotaire Bazile's *drapo* (cat. nos. 2 and 3), in the winged figures of Myrlande Constant's work, and in the title of that of Pascale Monnin, *L'Ange de la Résurrection*. This latter work, significantly, is suspended and reveals the image of wings from certain angles. The presence of a halo in the work by André Eugène is still more subtle. One can also be seen, as a crown, on Ezili's head in the painting by Voltaire Hector (cat. no. 14). In fact, artists past and present of all persuasions have

Illustration 1

Célestin Faustin
Mauvaise recherche, 1980
Acrylic on canvas,
60 x 95 cm.
Collection Choko.

drawn from this resource, including Hector Hyppolite (1894-1948); Jean-Claude Garoute, known as Tiga (1935-2006); Dieudonné Cédor (1925-2010); Rose-Marie Desruisseau (1933-1988); Jean-René Jérôme (1942-1991); Bernard Séjourné (1947-1994); Favrange Valcin, known as Valcin II (1947-2010); Jean Camille, known as Nasson (1961-2008); and Barbara Prézeau Stephenson (1965-).

This is the result of the salience of Christian imagery in Haiti's visual culture.[3] In fact, the imagery has been present in every segment of society since the colonial period. Obviously present in Catholic institutions, it was adopted by both public and domestic Vodou. Images of saints populate the altars of Vodou sanctuaries. They are painted on the walls of the *ounfò* (temples) and on sacred objects. They appear on ritual flags. Elements of certain ritual drawings (*vèvè*) are based on them, such as the heart of Mater Dolorosa in Ezili Freda's *vèvè* and Saint Jacques's sword and flag in that of Ogou (see cat. nos. 2 and 3).

The new creators of the 1940s and 1950s, particularly those who came to prominence without attending art school, turned to the iconographic and formal references available to them. These included illustrations from books, magazines, calendars, and advertising with Christian imagery. This was the case both for artists working with Vodou themes and for those who tackled Christian themes, like Philomé Obin. Artists expanded the number of biblical subjects: there are endless earthly paradises, Noah's arks, Crucifixions, Annunciations, Adorations of the Magi, saints, angels, and Madonnas. Religious ceremonies like weddings, baptisms, and funerals are relatively abundant. With respect to Vodou themes, representations of the *lwa* consistently, although not exclusively, feature the images of the corresponding saints. These entities may appear alone or in action in a cultural realm. Their interactions with their servitors are the subject of highly complex compositions, like those of Célestin Faustin (illustration 1).[4] The images are sometimes used "as is," drawn, painted, appended, or glued. A significant, distinctive element may be retained from the reference image. The latter is not always immediately recognizable, however, in the work of Robert Saint-Brice and artists from the Saint-Soleil movement. Religious imagery is sometimes summoned for subjects that are seemingly not religious, perhaps to provide a religious connotation to an event. For example, Philomé Obin, known for his historical works, painted the fall of President Élie Lescot in 1946. The head of state, perfectly recognizable,

Illustration 2

Marie-Hélène Cauvin
La Fléchée
45.72 x 76.20 cm
Ink, gouache and charcoal on paper, 2007
© 2007 Marie-Hélène Cauvin

is walking alone on a beach followed, or rather chased away, by an angel with a sword. Marine animals appear, swimming in the same direction as the president (to celebrate his departure?), and a thick cloud of angels' heads appears in the sky. The motif of the angel chasing away the president evokes that of the angel casting Adam and Eve from paradise in the eponymous work painted by Masaccio in 1425-1427 in the church of Santa Maria del Carmine.

Pascale Monnin's description of her *L'Ange de la Résurrection* provides us with another example of the use and possible interpretation of such imagery:

> It is the face of a child split by a diamond-studded fault line. The face teaches us the need to live with our scars, to make our stitches sparkling diamonds and to transform our wounds into weapons of mass construction.

> Living with our bruises, not like something we suffer through and hide, but like something that makes us more beautiful, deeper....

> The resurrection angel and the Phoenix reborn from its ashes are fighting the same battle!

Another example is *Marassa Andy and Basquiat* by Vladimir Cybil Charlier.[5] *Marasa* are twins in Haitian Creole. The artist translated the friendship of the two artists Andy Warhol and Jean-Michel Basquiat into the Haitian language of twinning using a chromolithograph of the saints Cosmas and Damian, the Catholic equivalents of the *lwa marasa*. In *La fléchée* (The Arrow, 2007), part of a series on gangs, Marie-Hélène Cauvin uses the image of Saint Sebastian (illustration 2) to tackle the subject of young martyred women, objects of exploitation in the ghettos.

It is important to note that the same images of Catholic saints that have been a source of creativity for artists have also been at the heart of a recurring conflict in Haiti. Priests have always denounced the appropriation of such images by Vodou. Paintings and sculptures have been removed from sacred sites because devotion to them was considered non-conforming. The leaders of the Catholic Church ordered the destruction of pious images found in the *ounfò* during the anti-superstition campaign of the early 1940s.[6] However, the visual arts movement, which came to life soon thereafter through the Centre d'Art (which opened in 1944), drew on this iconographic stock by playing with the layers of meaning deposited in it. The extent of change since then can be seen in the significant volume of *reinterpreted images of saints* that have taken over public spaces in cities like Port-au-Prince, on the walls, on signs of all kinds, and on public transport vehicles (the "tap tap").

THE IMAGINARIES OF ORALITURE

Iconographic resources and invention obviously exceed the boundaries of Catholic imagery. Other resources must be taken into account, including the imaginaries of oraliture. Myth, legends, fairy tales, and anecdotes are brought into play to varying degrees. They provide themes as well as registers for experimentation and interpretation with immense potential. They touch on the image of the artist, her or his sources of inspiration, the titles of works, their contents, and their status. Multiple narratives can be developed and redeveloped as needed.

Legendary stories have accompanied the introduction to the public of many artists, from Hector Hyppolite (1894-1948), to André Pierre (1914-2005), to Préfète Duffaut (1923-2012), to the artists of the Saint-Soleil movement of the 1970s. Such stories have also conditioned the reception of their works. The same thread seems to run through the stories; however, each case has its own significant specificities resulting from the artists' profiles, their personal histories, their own involvement in telling their legends, and from the links between the legends and their work. The artists appear as active agents in a system that involves both their creation and their discourse about it. The work sits at the heart of a co-mingling of stories running from those that nourished its conception to those that accompany its reception.

A painting by Hector Hyppolite, *Rêve d'un ange* (Angel's Dream, illustration 3), exemplifies what can result from linking reinterpreted or already re-semanticized Catholic imagery, parameters from a belief system, and personal legends (self-generated or generated in a situation of exchange then echoed by multiple voices).[7] At first glance, the work appears to illustrate one of the artist's most famous statements: that his inspiration comes from the *lwa*. At the center of the painting is a large winged figure presented in profile. Kneeling in front of a tree stump, the angel holds a tablet in his left hand with the following inscription: "VOICI. REVENIR LÉ RÉVE Dé la peinture sur Dé ma pansé Dans tout la nature… Hector Hyppolite."[8] There is a sword in front of the angel's knees. At the lower right side of the painting is a jug covered with a net decorated with porcelain beads and, to the left, a gourd enclosed in the same type of netting (an *ason* or sacred rattle), and a little bell. Above this appears the bust of a person, emerging from a cloud. To the left and above the head of that figure rise two motifs that could be a pair of wings. A little higher up, the artist has placed a quarter moon. A long vine with leaves and flowers closes off the top part of the composition to the right.

Illustration 3

Hector Hyppolite
Rêve d'un ange, c. 1947
Oil on masonite,
63 x 79 cm
Musée d'Art Haïtien du Collège
Saint-Pierre, Port-au-Prince

The title by which the painting is identified in the collection of the Musée d'Art Haïtien du Collège Saint-Pierre, *Rêve d'un ange*, interprets the inscription through a shortcut, necessarily incomplete, and with an ambiguity that does not do justice to the piece.[9] Is the angel dreaming or is this the dream of the other figure? It is most likely the other figure, emerging from the cloud, who is dreaming. By signing the text with the only signature on the painting, Hyppolite confirms that what is written there relates to him personally. He stages his relationship with the painting, suggesting that we see his own image in that of the dreamer. Given that the *lwa* are also known under the names *mistè* (mysteries), *sen* (saints), and *zanj* (angels) we might think that this is the incarnation of one of them — in this case, the one who announced a visit to Hyppolite that would mark a turning point in his life. If there were any doubts about the Vodou identity of the angel, the ritual objects are there to dissipate them. However, the bell and *ason* are objects that are symbolic of the *oungan* (male Vodou priest), and their presence appears to define the dreamer's status.[10] This is Hyppolite as an *oungan* dreaming in the moonlight of his future as a painter. The tablet is already a painting signed "Hector Hyppolite." The angel holds the tablet, admiring it and showing it to us so that we too can admire it, or, more to the point, to invite us to read and decipher it.

No indication is provided in the text as to the identity of the celestial being, although the inscription indicates that this is a recurring dream, like the manifestation of an obsession, an idea that occupies a thought, "my" thought signals Hyppolite. An angel as the figure of desire! So, rather than a *lwa*, it could be another entity. From the standpoint of Vodou, the person is constituted by several entities including the *kò kadav* (physical body), the *nanm* (soul), the *ti bonanj* (little soul), the *gwo bonanj* (big soul), and the *zetwal* (star). Ethnographic writings on Vodou over the past decades have stressed, in particular, the importance of the *ti bonanj* and *gwo bonanj*, even if the interpretation of their respective roles has varied over time from one author to the next. Guérin Montilus subscribes to the mobility of the *gwo bonanj*, which leaves the servitor at the moment of the epiphany, of possession by the *lwa*.[11] Alfred Métraux notes that, "our thoughts, memories and feelings — that is, our intellectual and emotional lives, depend on the *gwo bonanj*. It is closely associated with the body, which it only leaves during sleep to roam. What it sees and the adventures it has during its night wanderings are the stuff of our dreams."[12] On the other hand, for Carol de Lynch,[13] Max G. Beauvoir,[14] and Rachel Beauvoir and Didier Dominique[15] it is rather the *ti bonanj* that is mobile. It travels at the time of possession. It is the seat of knowledge, wisdom, and intelligence. Whether *gwo* or *ti bonanj*, Hyppolite stages in this painting the one that wanders and represents the principle of consciousness. He paints his *bonanj*, materializing his own thinking and desire.

A FEW MODES OF EXPRESSION

Hyppolite's painting demonstrates the use of an available iconographic reference in relation to the resources of oraliture. *Work* is done and the result, when compared to other pieces by the same artist and by his contemporaries, encourages us to push our characterization of such artistic production a bit further.

The *work* is a visual coding and/or recoding operation from which results pieces with formal qualities that enable their categorization other than by genre, trend, style, or subject matter. These works can be distinguished by narration, metamorphosis, presentification, and apparition.[16] These four modes of expression are not mutually exclusive. It is also possible to find others, but they especially manifest themselves autonomously and heteronomously. A mode of expression is autonomous when all of the constitutive elements of the image contribute to its specificity. There is heteronomy when the combined elements explicitly highlight the image's creative ambiguity.

Narration is the deployment of a representation suggesting a story. Recognizable elements are organized in such a way as to make linear reading possible. The work of Myrlande Constant falls in this category, as does the painting by Jean Charlemagne (cat. no. 5). Objects made from cut metal, the painting by Frantz Zéphirin (cat. no. 28), and that of Pauléus Vital (cat. no. 27) provide examples of metamorphoses in which human, animal, and plant shapes meet, combine, transform and mutate to give birth to composite beings and objects. Presentification consists in making an object or group of objects, or a figure or a group of figures present in and for themselves. This implies that all narrative systems must be self-contained. *La Sirène* (The Mermaid) by Serge Jolimeau (cat. no. 15) is not involved in any form of interaction. It exists for itself only. The same is true of *Brave Guede* by Gérard Valcin (cat. no. 26). His environment and the items surrounding him are only there to strengthen his identity or identification. The portrait of a man by Sacha Tebó (cat. no. 25) is also an example of presentification. However, the way the body is handled, some parts of which fuse with the background, also uses the mode of apparition. In this case, there is a real presence, but for an instant only. It is a fugitive, fleeting phenomenon that should not be *presentified*. The challenge consists in suggesting the fleetingness, the imminence of a disappearance. From this standpoint, the work of Mario Benjamin articulates presentification and apparition in the same way as that of Tebó. However, several artists thematize apparition as such or use processes related to it. The apparition of Ezili is, in fact, the subject of Voltaire Hector's painting (cat. no. 14).

In the approach taken by the artists of Saint-Soleil — represented in the collection by Prosper Pierre-Louis (cat. nos. 21 and 22), Levoy Exil (cat. no. 12), and Louisiane Saint Fleurant (cat. no. 23) — narration does not appear as a familiar or current method. The work of these artists primarily reflects the three other modes, both autonomously and heteronomously. The artists of Saint-Soleil share a formal vocabulary and stylistic processes. Among them, a central, ever-present element is a circular or ovoid shape that may be *a head, a face, a mask, a solar disk, or a figure.* It usually has two "eyes," small, globular shapes, which are essential, as can be seen in the special care given to them compared to the nose and mouth in many cases. These eyes pierce or punctuate the paintings, conferring a presence to the figures and ensuring a degree of vitality to the compositions. There are also entities that suggest the shape of a bird and of plants with branches, leaves, and flowers. The treatment of these elements, their shaping and positioning in a spatial context, is done with a network of lines delimiting the application of color. The basic structure and overall configuration rest on the relaxed, vigorous or tight, simple or complex interplay of lines and colors (when the painting is not done in black and white).

This formal and stylistic approach does not promote narration. The potential for self-generation of shapes through the interplay of lines facilitates the exploration of metamorphosis. The presence of a central figure (multipliable), omnipresent, *head-face-mask-solar disk*, caught in linear and colored webs, provides an opportunity to experiment, search for, or reach presentification and apparition. What strikes the viewer first in Louisiane Saint Fleurant's work is the *presence*, not its evocation or suggestion, but a clearly defined presence. The face belongs to a body, not to an evanescent shape, not to a suggested thickness ready to melt into the colored networks of lines, but a real body, with weight, recognizable as such. A body that is often accompanied by other bodies. In fact, figures. Adults. Children. Alone. Or interacting. Compared to the figure or figures, the other elements of the common vocabulary brought together, while symbolically or decoratively important, appear to be quite secondary: birds or other animals, or houses, sometimes barely visible, but virtually omnipresent. Branches and leaves are more obvious and join the inevitable linear and colored networks. These elements do not subsume and only rarely dilute the figures who are completely detached from them. This excludes or limits the potential for metamorphosis. The artist does not intend to structure the pictorial space by deploying a continuous network of shapes with which bodies, beings, or undefinable, unnamable entities would join, fuse, or be juxtaposed. Saint Fleurant's main concern is to make figures present. This is why she gives them special treatment, starting with their proportions, which generally take up nearly the entire canvas. She wants us to see them, with their globular eyes, preferably standing facing us. A comparison with photography sheds light on their solemn pose; they are unable to take their eyes off the lens of the camera. To be present. The fixed, immobile stare becomes searching, questioning. These figures, which she can render entirely autonomous like objects in clay, call out to us and invite us to a one-on-one meeting.

TECHNIQUES AND MATERIALS: THE PATHS TO RENEWAL

The above analyses concern both established trends and the new scene. However, works by artists of this new scene are different in many ways. Volume and space have become a greater preoccupation than before. The different scales explored in the conception of works/objects immediately invite artists to imagine their locations in space. It is primarily in installations that spatial parameters are conceived as an integral aspect of creation. Performance involves temporality and direct interaction with the public as well. The importance of volumetric objects is particularly striking. Although we recognize known materials (wood, stone, metal, concrete, etc.), exploration of the possibilities of assembly and of recovery has overturned the order of things. The field of possibilities has been significantly broadened, in terms of both the materials that can be used and the techniques and know-how that can be brought to bear. The transfer of know-how from one artist to another (involving confrontations, juxtapositions, and sharing) is one of the foundations of this new scene and one of the impulses behind its creativity. The decisive phenomenon of this new movement is the potential of subjecting materials and techniques to experimentation.

Myrlande Constant, whose works occupy a prominent position in *drapo vodou* creation, has achieved this by an indirect route. She did not emerge from a workshop that produced *drapo*. In fact, her technique is completely different from that used in the workshops. She does not sew sequins or pearls on fabric; she uses the technique known as *perlage*.[17] She executes her motifs using a threading method with a crochet hook (and not a needle like others) with the back of the piece facing her (that is, she cannot immediately see the work taking shape, contrary to the method of other *drapo* artists). She learned the technique from her mother, who worked in a factory that subcontracted the manufacture of beaded items, notably wedding dresses. After working in the factory, she began to use the technique to create works similar to *drapo vodou*.

When Constant began executing this technique, the ritual objects known as *drapo vodou* had already entered a phase of dynamic transformation due to their commercialization. The production of clearly recognizable items not intended for religious purposes was growing.[18] A new iconography was deployed, sometimes going beyond the boundaries of Vodou symbolism. In many cases, figurative painting was used as the model, giving rise to all types of narrative scenes. Edouard Duval-Carrié had a number of his paintings reproduced by specialists of this type of work. Given these changes, applied to this new category of works, the name *drapo vodou* has become purely generic and refers both to the original ritual uses of the objects and to the techniques used. Artists like Lhérisson Dubréus and David Boyer have followed in the footsteps of Pierrot Barra and continued the transformations by introducing found objects in the *drapo*. Boyer has replaced sequins with buttons that he juxtaposes with other objects such as recovered electronics circuits, and often adds motifs (faces, human and animals shapes) in hand-embossed metal.

And the experimentation does not stop there. Sequins are used extensively, as seen in the works of Vladimir Cybil Charlier (illustration 4) and Guyodo (Frantz Jacques) (illustration 5). The latter uses imported second-hand clothes (*pèpè*, as they are called in Haiti) with these elements, which he cuts and applies to volumetric objects or flat surfaces. It is primarily the glittering effect that counts most. These are the same effects sought by Killy (Patrick Ganthier) (illustrations 6 and 7), using a completely different process. He applies on paper a pictorial composite that recreates the glossy and sparkling effects of sequins. This concern is related to the search for a sort of kinetic effect explored by a number of artists. It manifests itself in the use of pieces of mirror, marbles, glass, and other shiny objects found in many works. Lionel St.-Eloi (illustrations 8 and 9) cuts aluminum sheets to make small pieces of a more or less regular shape. The pieces are then attached to each other to cover a structure, sometimes of large dimensions. The result is a surface that looks like fish scales and recalls sequins sown together. Many pieces of mirror are added, producing multiple reflections. They change depending on the angle and distance from which the onlooker is standing. In addition to pearls, jewelry, and sometimes mirrors, Pascale Monnin introduces the mobility of suspended works that play with light and/or a lighting system that

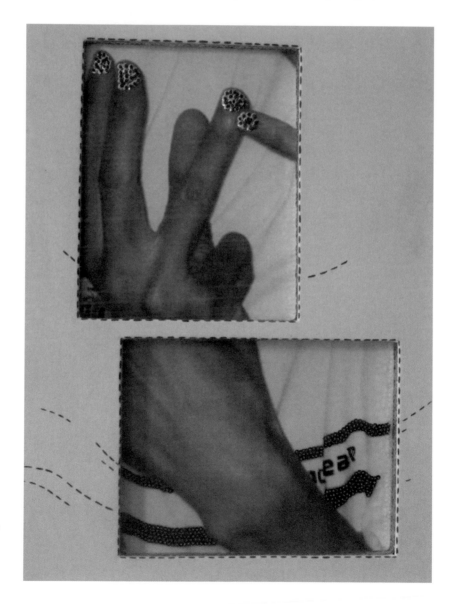

Illustration 4

Vladimir Cybil Charlier
V for victory,
Acrylic, canvas, photographic
print, sequins and beads
30 x 34 x 2 in. (70.25cm x
86.50cm x 5cm)
© Vladimir Cybil Charlier

adds additional "vitality" through the interplay of shadows projected by the works.

The kinetic effect, which I consider an extension of the changes to *drapo vodou* discussed above, is one of the multiple types of experimentation undertaken by the artists of this new scene. Note that the analyses on which this text has focused are only meant to be suggestive. The goal was to highlight a few points that may not be sufficiently emphasized when discussing the dynamic nature of visual arts creation in Haiti. In the end, the transformations observed invite the reader to understand metamorphosis in a broader sense than that of one mode of expression among others. Let us say that there are likely several registers, including the principles of the potential transformation of beings and things in beliefs, the multiple stories of oraliture, and phenomena like possession. These principles are also at work in the ways of understanding, appropriating, and interpreting signs, symbols, and images in circulation. This means that there is a system of meaning creation, one of society's sources of creativity, which is particularly lively in subaltern milieus. The creative act, which is available to everyone, remains malleable. The potential for exploration is still wide open.

Illustration 5

Guyodo
Saint Jacques, 2009
Recycled glass and textiles
41 x 19.5 13 inches

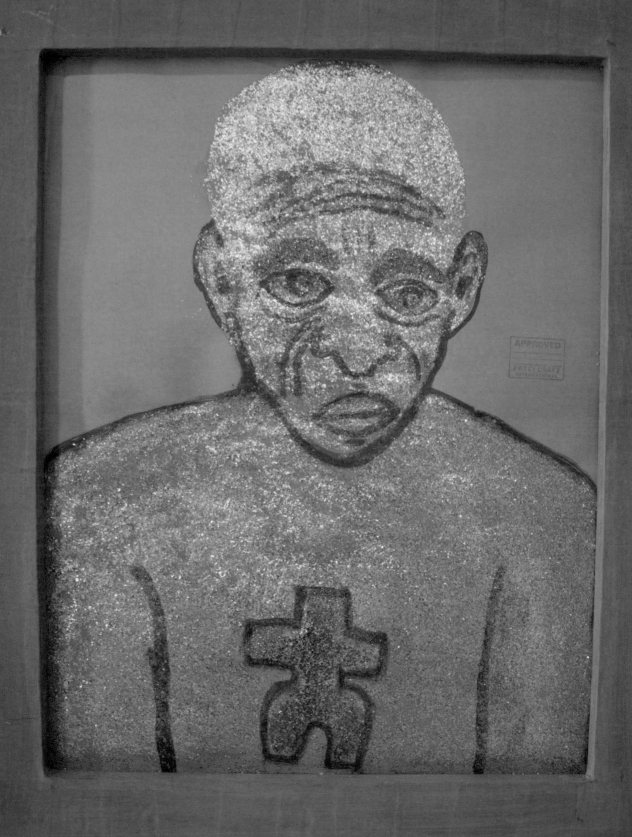

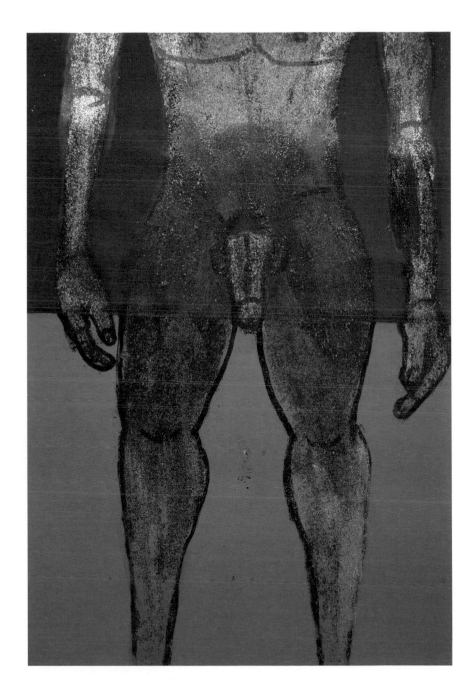

Illustrations 6 and 7

Killy (Patrick Ganthier)

LEFT:

A work from the series
Croix des Bossales (2009-2011)
56 x 71 cm
pellicules brillantes on cardboard
Photographed by Carlo A. Célius
in May 2013 at Les Ateliers Jérôme,
Pétionville, Haiti

RIGHT:

Detail of a work from the series
Croix des Bossales (2009-2011)
168 x 71 cm
pellicules brillantes on cardboard
Photographed by Carlo A. Célius
in May 2013 at the artist's studio,
Pétionville, Haiti

© Carlo A. Célius

Illustrations 8 and 9

Lionel St-Eloi
La déesse des astres
Photos by Carlo A.Célius
at l'Institut Français d'Haïti
in November 2013.
© 2013 Carlo A. Célius

[1]Editors' note: We have translated "*création plastique*" as "visual art" throughout the essay.

[2]Oraliture includes discursive forms such as legends, myths, tales, proverbs, riddles, magico-religious formulas, prayers, different types of songs, maxims, stories, etc. The concept, which is well known in the world of francophone literature, was first proposed by Haitian writer Ernst Mirville, also known as Pierre Bambou, in 1974 (Pierre Bambou, "Le concept d'oraliture," *Le Nouvelliste*, May 12, 1974). He returned to it several years later, offering clarifications in an interview with Pierre-Raymond Dumas (Pierre-Raymond Dumas, "Interview sur le concept d'oraliture accordée à Pierre-Raymond Dumas par le docteur Ernest Mirville," *Conjonction* nos. 161-162 [March-June 1984]: 161-164). Maximilien Laroche, for whom oraliture is a great inspiration, shows how much more productive it is than the concept of oral literature. Laroche specifies that the necessity of distinguishing oraliture and literature and of considering their parallel evolutions does not exclude the possibility of utilizing the same methodological approaches to analyze them. These are two modes of creation that are not mutually exclusive. Maximilien Laroche, *La double scène de la représentation: Oraliture et littérature dans la Caraïbe* (Quebec City: GRELCA, Université Laval, coll. "Essais," no 8, 1991).

[3]See Carlo A. Célius, "L'imagerie chrétienne dans la création plastique d'Haïti," *Histoire, Monde et Cultures religieuses* 29 (2014): 143-172.

[4]Carlo A. Célius, "Célestin Faustin, un peintre haïtien face au sacré," *Histoire et missions chrétiennes* 12 (December 2009): 93-110.

[5]Reproduced in *Small Axe* 9/2, no. 18 (September 2005): 53.

[6]See Kate Ramsey's *The Spirits and the Law: Vodou and Power in Haiti* (Chicago: The University of Chicago Press, 2011) on the history of sanctions against Vodou. On the anti-superstition campaign of the early 1940s see Lewis Ampidu Clorméus, "Entre l'État, les élites et les religions en Haïti. Redécouvrir la campagne antisuperstitieuse de 1939-1942," Ph.D. dissertation, École des Hautes Études en Sciences Sociales/Université d'Etat d'Haïti, 2012.

[7]See Carlo A. Célius, "Hector Hyppolite, l'insolite," *Recherches en esthétique* 16 (October 2010): 167-173. For further reading on other aspects of the work of Hyppolite from the same perspective, see Carlo A. Célius, "The Creator's Vèvè," in *Mystical Imagination. The Art of Haitian Master Hector Hyppolite* (Washington, D.C.: Haitian Art Society, 2013), 42-55; "Les vèvè du créateur," in *Hector Hyppolite* (Paris: Éditions de Capri, 2011), 67-98; "Hector Hyppolite: ruse et subversion," *Le Nouvelliste* (September 18, 2008).

[8]At first glance, the words "Dans tout" might appear to be the single word "Pandant." However, the first letter is clearly a D, as confirmed by a comparison with the D above (in "Dé ma pansé") and the "p's" in "Hyppolite."

[9]See *Le Musée d'Art Haïtien Saint Pierre* (1983; Port-au-Prince, 1995).

[10]Note that the taking of the *ason* is one of the means of access to the status known as *oungan asogwe*. In his autobiographical story, as reconstructed by Thoby-Marcelin, Hyppolite does not introduce himself as an *oungan asogwe*. He does not imply that he practiced any form of public Vodou — that is, at an *ounfò* (temple) attended by a community of "servitors" where regular "*services*" (ceremonies) are held, some of which are open to the public. Philippe Thoby-Marcelin and Jean Chenet, "La

double vie d'Hector Hyppolite, artiste et prêtre vodou (excerpts)," *Conjonction* 16 (August 1948): 40-44, and 17 (October 1948): 37-41. However, Lucien Price and Michel-Philippe Lerebours note that the artist did in fact have an *ounfò*, but that it was in Port-au-Prince. Hyppolite left Saint-Marc, where he lived before he met Thoby-Marcelin, to move to the capital once his membership in the Centre d'Art was approved. Two photos — one reproduced in *Haiti: art naïf, art vaudou*, ed. Jean-Marie Drot (Rome: Edizioni Carte Segrete, 1988), and another in *Hector Hyppolite* (Paris: Éditions de Capri, 2011) — show Hyppolite standing in what appears to be a corner of his house holding an *ason* and bell. Behind him to the left is a small table on which there are several items. There is a cross and four or five chromolithographs of Catholic saints. At present, I am only aware of this image confirming Hyppolite's *oungan* status. Hyppolite poses as an *oungan asogwe* in these pictures, which should be associated with the painting *Rêve d'un ange*.

[11] Guérin Montilus, "Vodun and Social Transformation in the African Diasporic Experience: The Concept of Personhood in Haitian Vodun Religion" in *Vodou in Haitian Life and Culture: Invisible Powers*, eds. Claudine Michel and Patrick Bellegarde-Smith (New York: Palgrave MacMillan, 2006), 1-6. Joan (now Colin) Dayan notes that while it is generally accepted that according to the concept of the body in Vodou self-awareness retreats to allow a *lwa* to enter, consciousness is never fully erased. Joan Dayan, *Haiti, History, and the Gods* (1995; Berkeley: University of California Press,1998), 68.

[12] Alfred Métraux, *Le vaudou haïtien* (1958; Paris, Gallimard, 1984), 139.

[13] Carol de Lynch, *Le cahier sacré du vodouisant* (Port-au-Prince: Éditions Deschamps, 2008), 170.

[14] Max G. Beauvoir, "Herbs and Energy: The Holistic Medical System of the Haitian People," in *Vodou in Haitian Life and Culture: Invisible Powers*, eds. Claudine Michel and Patrick Bellegarde-Smith (New York: Palgrave Macmillan, 2006), 112-133.

[15] Rachel Beauvoir and Didier Dominique, *Savalou E* (Montreal: Les Éditions du Cidihca, 2003), 90-91.

[16] A number of authors have evoked the idea of metamorphosis with regard to a given artist, work, or even type of creation. See for example, Patrice Dilly and Philippe Bernard, *Métamorphoses, sculptures et fers des Bòsmetal d'Haïti* (La Roque d'Anthéron: Vents d'ailleurs, 2004). For me, it is a question of one modality among others. And as this essay examines, the possible extended use of this characterization is not limited to transformations resulting from practices of recycling.

[17] The technique of beaded embroidery derives from the embroidery of Lunéville, which appeared in nineteenth century France, and consisted of imitating certain kinds of lacework by embroidering on netting. It still exists in countries with low-wage labor where there are workshops employing "petites mains," that is, those engaged as embroiderers and beaders who execute motifs destined for the houses of haute couture. See Nicole Vulser, "Les Indiens, petites mains du luxe," *Le Monde* (September 7, 2012).

[18] For more about *drapo vodou*, see the following works (among others): Tina Girouard, *Sequin Artists of Haiti* (New Orleans: Contemporary Arts Center of New Orleans, 1994); Patrick Arthur Polk, *Haitian Vodou Flags* (Jackson: University Press of Mississippi, 1997); Nancy Josephson, *Spirits in Sequins: Vodou Flags of Haiti* (Atglen: Schiffer Publishing Ltd, 2007).

PICTURES FROM HEAVEN: TRANSFORMATIVE VISIONS *AND HAITIAN DIASPORIC* ARTISTIC PRACTICES

Jerry Philogene

Haiti is not that weird. It is the fiction of Haitian exceptionalism that is weird.[1]

Why, I wonder, in a country of such hypnotic beauty, with a climate as lucent as southern Italy's and a people favored with leisure, is the art of painting practically moribund? Why, in this haunting city of 150,000 inhabitants, rich in history, literally shimmering with color and charm, is there no single art gallery, no art shop, not even a nook where a painting can be hung for people to see? [2]

I began conceptualizing this essay on the beautiful and historically complex island of Barbados while working at the interdisciplinary art space, Fresh Milk Art Platform. What captivated me besides the pastoral landscape filled with cows, roosters, and sleeping dogs was the series of conversations asking how to define Barbadian art. What are the iconographies that represent Barbadian art? Who has the privilege to define Barbadian art? Who can be included in local and international exhibitions, and who has the right to choose those who are included and those who are excluded from these often career-advancing exhibitions? During the conversations, I was reminded that these deep-rooted and deeply troubling issues occur not only in the context of Haiti and Haitian art, but also in other artistic communities that have not had the privilege of defining their own creative productions and art histories.

In one of his most influential and thought-provoking essays, "The Odd and the Ordinary: Haiti, the Caribbean, and the World" — from which the first epigraph of this essay is drawn — Michel-Rolph Trouillot points out that Haiti has been positioned as "unique, bizarre, unnatural, odd, queer, freakish, or grotesque," and therefore unexplainable, and that "special…modes of investigation applicable to other societies are not relevant here."[3] Trouillot's essay asks what accounts for this special status in Western narrative. Is it because Haiti is the "eldest daughter of France and Africa?"[4] Is it because of Haiti's specific political history, or is it because former European colonizers and U.S. occupiers defined their sense of racial superiority against Haiti, which they perceived as a definitive marker of blackness? The second epigraph highlights DeWitt

Peters's musings, recounting what has often been cited as the *decisive* moment when "Haitian art" was conceived. On a balcony in Pétionville in 1943, Peters, one of the co-founders of the Centre d'Art, wonders why in such an "extraordinary" environment Haitians had not been able to produce a sustainable artistic community. It is unclear to which Haiti "favored with leisure" Peters referred: the Haiti that was slowly recovering from the 19-year American occupation, or the Haiti that was languishing under the repressive government of Élie Lescot?

I begin with these two passages in order to signal the ways in which discussions about Haitian art have long been framed and continually narrated. The latter reinforces a fascination with Haiti, wondering, in a country with such "hypnotic beauty," why there are no public venues to display such visual richness, no creative outlets for those "blessed" with leisure. Peters's musing probes Haiti's special appeal, while at the same time speculating about its odd cultural infrastructure and lack of artistic production. The former critiques the characterization of Haiti as unique, bizarre, and oddly freakish. Trouillot argues that it is instead the exceptionalism attributed to Haiti that must be interrogated and problematized.

I offer in the next pages what I hope are ways to consider Haitian art in a broader and more expansive fashion. Following Trouillot, I demonstrate that modern and contemporary Haitian art is not exceptional but rather is part of an engagement with black Atlantic visual aesthetics and culture. Similarly to the exhibition itself, I explore a captivating mix of emerging voices and well-established artists, some of whose works illustrate traditional Haitian cultural motifs and creative styles, while other works reflect a complex interplay among material, space, style, and form characteristic of the global art world.

What follows is a brief exploration of selected works by artists who represent various generations and prolific artistic movements that have transcended national boundaries and are part of black Atlantic aesthetic practices. What these artists share beyond their cultural and ethnic heritage is a desire to illustrate a tradition of craft and fine art that is not borne of a singular school or hermetic aesthetic discourse but instead is engaged with multiple realities. These realities are not "odd" or "exceptional." They are ordinary and intrinsic to transnational, cross-cultural, and parallel dialogues that might begin in Haiti and continue in New York, Boston, Miami, the Bahamas, Curaçao, and Geneva or perhaps in Paris, Berlin, Senegal.

Volumes have been written about Haitian art that are replete with essays featuring images of quaint scenes from daily life and the market place, lush flora, exotic birds and flamingos, and religious ceremonies and iconography rendering these depictions as transhistorical absolutes. Many of the artworks in this exhibition depict the kinds of visual iconographies that have cemented Haitian art within an "intuitive," "naïve," or "primitive" taxonomy. Such designations situate works such as Préfète Duffaut's *Troisième Tentation* (cat. no. 9), Gesner Abelard's *Birds and Foliage* (cat. no. 1), Jean René Chery's *Skipping Rope* (cat. no. 6), and Voltaire Hector's *Manbo a ap fe apel a Erzulie Freda li ap vini* (cat. no. 14) within an over-simplified understanding of Haiti as a place "where art is joy." Nonetheless, the range of artistic perspectives in this exhibition attempts to map out the critical and artistic pathways between Haiti and its diaspora, bringing together artists who engage, challenge, and contribute to local and global art discourses using traditional and formal, as well as non-traditional and non-formal art practices. Paintings, drawings, and sculptures made from conventional and non-conventional materials present an evocative balance of, on the one hand, works inspired by the religiosity that has been a cultural bedrock of modern Haitian art and culture and, on the other hand, contemporary pieces that are invested in transgressive postmodern art approaches to media and aesthetics. As such, *Transformative Visions* allows for the possibility of new conversations that encompass artistic traditions and global art histories to define art produced by people of Haitian descent in ways not limited by the taxing and overgeneralized descriptor "Haitian art." The artworks require viewers to rethink what they may have understood to be Haitian art. It is precisely here in this creative space of the gallery that we view the range of cross-cultural influences fashioned within transnational contexts deeply rooted in and inflected by Haitian cultural specificity and black diasporic cosmopolitanism.

The complex pictorial narrative presented in the densely worked surface of Myrlande Constant's richly patterned and detailed *drapo Points Saint Miel* (cat. no. 7) illustrates this mélange of cultural and historical influences. Many individuals populate the imaginative landscape of Constant's beautifully sequined and beaded tableau; the living, the recently dead, the long dead, and the resurrected take center stage under the sacred *mapou* tree. Constant's use of vivid imagery and evocation of spiritual folktales have established her as one of the most respected *drapo* makers in Haiti, garnering national and international recognition. Using images from daily life replete with religious and cultural symbolism, Constant employs the imagistic style of storytelling to illustrate activities under the *mapou* tree. The Saint Miel spirits as well as angels and the Gede *lwa* watch over the living and the dead, with Bawon Samdi symbolized by the black cross. Constant's piece recalls Clotaire Bazile's highly decorative *drapo* (cat. nos. 2 and 3) with their rich colors, vibrant textured patterns, and glittering beads and sequins celebrating Erzulie Freda, Dambala Ouedo, and Saint Jacques le Majeur. In Bazile's *drapo*, the printed images of Our Lady of Sorrows and Saint Jacques le Majeur speak elegantly to the syncretic visual relationship between Vodou and Roman Catholicism. Similarly, Constant's *drapo vodou* are rooted in an expressive tradition that explores the symbiotic relationship between the spiritual and secular.

Displayed in *ounfò* (Vodou temples) and incorporating the colors and *vèvè* specific to *lwa*, *drapo* have been part of traditional religious and artistic practice in Haiti for decades, influencing contemporary artists ranging from *drapo*-maker Mireille Delice who was trained by Constant, to U.S.-based Vladimir Cybil Charlier in her works *Ogoun X* (1996, illustration 1) and *Billie Zulie* (1997, illustration 2). Cybil's assemblages draw similarities between African American revolutionary leader Malcolm X and fierce Haitian Vodou warrior Ogou/Saint Jacques le Majeur, and between the beautiful and sultry African

Illustration 1

Vladimir Cybil Charlier
Ogoun X, 1996
Private collection

Illustration 2

Vladimir Cybil Charlier
Billie Zulie, 1997
© 1997
Vladimir Cybil Charlier

American songstress Billie Holiday and Vodou goddess of love and fertility, Erzulie Freda. In these two pieces — small box-like structures decorated with sequins, beads, and fabric — Cybil used an image of the body of Saint Jacques le Majeur with sword in hand and replaced his face with that of Malcolm X. She placed an image of Holiday on top of the body of Our Lady of Sorrows/Erzulie Freda. This synthesis of cultural traditions and symbolic icons in Cybil's as well as Constant's pieces illustrates the influence of a black Atlantic aesthetic while paying homage to the traditions of *drapo*-making.

At the 2009 Ghetto Biennale, Jamaican artist Ebony G. Patterson created the site-specific installation *Untitled: Haitian Flag Project* featuring her familiar images of young black men from her *Gangstas for Life* series (2008-) and influenced by the iconography of Haitian *lwa* that sport their own black Atlantic "bling" (illustration 3). The official blog of the National Gallery of Jamaica describes the installation:

> [R]eferencing Erzili Danto, Erzili Freda, Ren Kongo, Ayida Wedo and the Marasas...the foundational images had been printed on fabric and she worked with a Haitian Vodou flag maker to sequin and otherwise embellish them, effectively turning them into *drapos* dedicated to each of these *loas*. The five large *drapos* were installed, along with traditional and not-so-traditional offerings for the *loas* in question, inside the main room of one of the Grande [*sic*] Rue dwellings for a one-day exhibition. The installation captured the splendor of the sacred arts of Haitian Vodou and the bling aesthetic of contemporary gangsta culture, provocatively merged, and interrogated the spiritual and the material, the male and female, the traditional and the contemporary, and the Haitian and the Jamaican.[5]

What Patterson, Bazile, and Constant share is an understanding of the importance of splendor and beauty that is part of a black diasporic aesthetic tradition as well as a tactile expressivity that unabashedly celebrates both the spiritual and the worldly self.

Displaying diverse creative practices, *Transformative Visions* highlights the mixed-media mobile installation by Pascale Monnin (cat. no. 20). What is visually striking about this piece is its stylish use of beads, faux crystals, and pearls that are combined with steel wire to create a kinetic sculpture. Since 2006, Monnin has been using raku as part of her art-making process to create the masks that grace her mobile installations. Raku, a traditional Japanese pottery-making form, requires varying degrees of manipulation in temperature and glazing. In 2000, she began casting the faces of friends and family to explore the dualities of life and death and to capture the facial expressiveness of her sitters. Evoking the beauty of ruins and the possibilities of resurrection, *L'Ange de la Résurrection* features the facial mold of a young boy, Antoine, spreading his bejeweled wings. Slightly off center, a jewel-encrusted scar runs the length of Antoine's facial molded form. She says:

> I always love to play with the scar; at one point, the piece fell and instead of gluing the face back, I didn't want to hide that it had been broken so I glued it back together and put the beads on the part that had been cracked. I completely integrated this thing that happened to it into the material, into the piece. In part, that is what the piece is about, all that happens to us we integrate into something else and then it becomes more interesting. The piece talks about the scar and how we have to make sense of the pain and disillusionment of life.[6]

Her desire is not to create an exact replica of the sitter; rather, her goal is to capture the expression of the sitter at the precise moment his face shapes the mold. Departing from traditional portraiture created in the conventional media of paints, inks, and oils on canvas or paper, Monnin has created a body of work using surplus wedding accoutrements purchased from a defunct bridal store and found objects. She plays creatively with the style and perception of portraiture and image-making while exploring the sculptural form with diverse materials.

Illustration 3

Ebony G. Patterson
Untitled (Haitian Flag Project),
2009
© 2009 Ebony G. Patterson

Monnin's *L'Ange de la Résurrection* hangs elegantly from the ceiling and operates in the round, allowing for a full view of the sitter's head. As it spins, we see the back of the mask, an intricate and beautiful assemblage of beads, faux pearls and crystals, steel, and wires, disrupting the physical space of the gallery as light passes through the steel and wires to produce shadows on the gallery walls. Provocatively blending the elements of craft and fine arts, Monnin has created a sculptural piece that delicately shifts and flows in space to explore the continuum between spirituality and disillusionment, elements that are fundamental to the black diasporic experience.

Hundreds of miles away, on another continent, the Helsinki-born artist of Haitian and Swiss descent Sasha Huber uses discarded wood and staples to create a series of large-scale portraits. Her on-going series *Shooting Back: Reflections on Haitian Roots*, begun in 2004, consists of three portraits of individuals who have shaped the history of Haiti: Christopher Columbus, François Duvalier, and his son Jean-Claude Duvalier (illustrations 4 and 5). Using a semi-automatic staple gun, she punctured the rough surface of the discarded maple and birch panels with approximately 100,000 staples. In doing so, she allows our eyes to focus on the coarseness of the wood as well as the beauty in the shimmer reflecting off the staples, producing a work of art that is rich in history and in texture. Like Huber, who challenges the assumptions that portraits are "truthful" representations of their subjects, Monnin explores the aesthetic possibilities of non-traditional materials and their power to signify. She does so through fine artistry and a keen sense of spatial alignment of delicately balanced components, thereby operating in the realm of kinetic sculpture originated by American sculptor Alexander Calder.

The intricacies and results of mixing disparate materials are also explored in Florine Demosthene's sensuous drawings and paintings. Demosthene writes of her series *The Capture*:

> I've been intrigued by the black female body in contemporary visual culture and I'm piqued by how her

physical size is suppose[d] to dictate a certain set of ideals and behavior. Borrowing from Jonathan Swift's *Gulliver's Travels*, I chronicled my journey through the Caribbean and West Africa in a series of drawings entitled, *The Capture*. These mix[ed] media pieces, textual mélanges of ink, oil, graphite and charcoal, depict voluptuous female figures amid a strange world of decay and destruction. *The Capture* is the initial phase to constructing a non-typical black female heroine persona. By delving into the subconscious mind of a fictitious black heroine and the ephemeral quality of her thoughts and experiences, *The Capture* is an attempt to structure a new mythology that explores black female sexuality and sensuality.[7]

Her piece *Assed Out* (cat. no. 8), featuring the full side view of a nude voluptuous woman, exemplifies the portrayal of just such a "non-typical black female heroine." This unnamed central figure looks away from the viewer; with her derrière conspicuously displayed, her gaze is turned inward, as well as towards the houses and other figures in the background.

Demosthene's use of muted monochromatic colors blurs the figure and ground distinction. The materiality of the piece comes through in the painterly lushness of the central figure as well as in the richness of the subject matter. Through her placement of the black female body (and an occasional male figure) at the center of the setting, Demosthene has created a series that offers the possibility of rethinking the multiple spaces occupied by black women, particularly those who do not fall within normative notions of beauty, sensuality, and sexuality. The idea for this series began to take shape in her mind after a trip to Ghana in 2010. "I had been journaling all the way through," she states,

> so I just started by extracting sentences or phrases from my journal. I thought I should do drawings based upon all of this stuff that I'm seeing. And I was also really looking at doing something that could span ten years, and it can

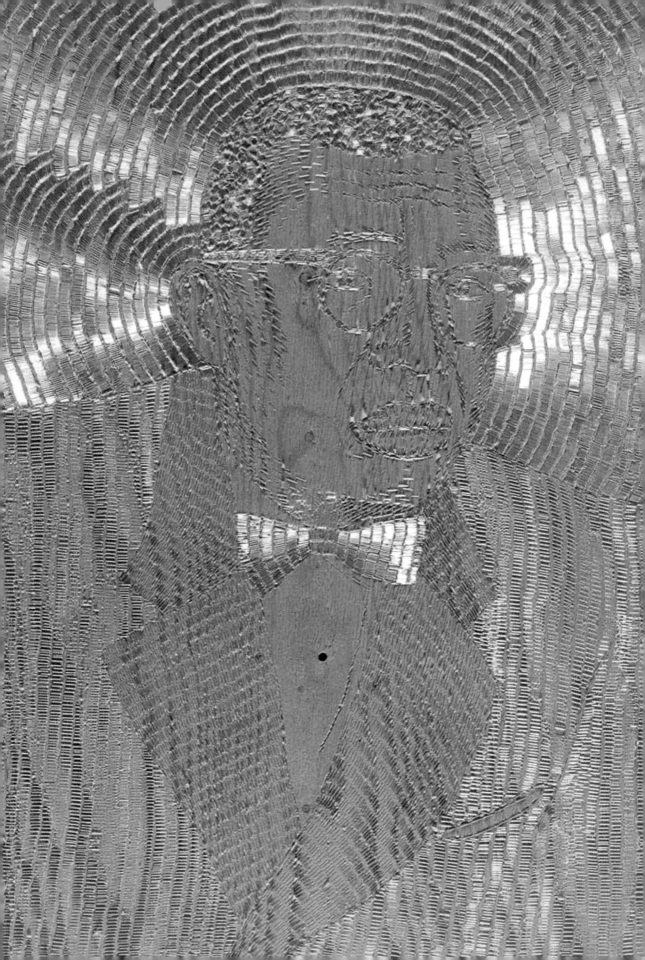

Illustration 4 and 5

Sasha Huber

LEFT:

Francois "Papa Doc" Duvalier
2004
metal staples on abandoned wood
Private collection, Paris
© 2004 Sasha Huber

RIGHT:

Jean-Claude "Baby Doc" Duvalier
2004
metal staples on abandoned wood
Collection of Botkyrka Konsthall,
Botkyrka municipality, Sweden
© 2004 Sasha Huber

go into a variety of different materials, so it…had to be very expansive…. I came up with this idea of this feminine… heroine. So, at the first stage I wondered what would go through her mind when she discovers she has these special abilities. That is how the series began.[8]

Through her manipulation of materials, the unpredictable results of their combination, and the chemical reaction of the oil, ink, graphite, and charcoal on the waxy surface of polypropylene, Demosthene explores the textured complexities of corporeality, as both formal analysis and aesthetic endeavor. Her exploration of the black female form is similar to the photographic work of Martinican Shirley Ruffin, whose manipulation of the formal and technical qualities of photography creates seductive imagery to highlight the medium's expressive and conceptual possibilities. Demosthene's bold embrace of the interplay between a tabooed subject, such as the black female nude, and the aesthetic quality of materials enables her to explore the visceral spaces between representation and abstraction, between belonging and alterity. Her work questions what it means to exist in a social world where your body does not fit into clearly defined hegemonic frameworks of beauty and desire. Evocative uses of the female body to theorize notions of gender, beauty, and femininity have been powerfully employed by late Cuban-American artist Ana Mendieta and African American artists such as Carrie Mae Weems, Lorna Simpson, and Mickalene Thomas, among others. By inserting the racialized female body as both protagonist and antagonist within the representational frame, they share with Demosthene the use of the female body to question the simultaneous visibility/invisibility that is signaled by her race, physicality, and sexuality. While her recent oeuvre does not solely focus on the issue of gender, I read Demosthene's work as part of a black womanist engagement with the meaning and representational strategy of the body, self-identity, sensuality, and community.

Internationally renowned artist Edouard Duval-Carrié creates paintings, drawings, sculptures, mixed-media pieces, and site-specific installations. Prolific, he moves freely between these diverse media and has thus created an extensive and rich body of work. Duval-Carrié has been the subject of many national and international monographic exhibitions including *Imagined Landscapes*, mounted in 2014 by the Pérez Art Museum in Miami. He is an astute student of history and culture and his paintings are multilayered provocative interplays between history, material, and process. Drawing from Haitian historical images and iconography, from the picturesque and allegorical imagery of North American and European paintings, and from African-derived religious symbolism, Duval-Carrié often encases his *lwa* in resin and thick layers of acrylic as they travel the causeways of Miami, traverse the watery forested island of Ginen, and spend time in Fort Dimanche. In *Trois Feuilles* (cat. no. 10), three *lwa* from the *Migration of the Spirit* that often appear in his paintings occupy the center panel of his triptych. With an effective use of visual language, he has created a thoughtful and stimulating body of work that comes from a personal place yet has universal appeal. He places painting at the center of his artistic practice while challenging its tenets, as is illustrated in the sculptural elements of his work: hand-made ornate frames, thickly applied acrylic and resin on canvas, and paintings rendered on metal with glitter glue. His deft use of materials creates beautiful pieces that combine the rich history of Haiti with its spiritual depth and artistic traditions. His work has consistently maintained the fecund symbolism of the African-derived religion of Vodou coupled with, at times, overt political consciousness. Through his process-based work, he has explored themes ranging from spirituality to the experience of diaspora and dislocation, all the while subtly critiquing contemporary implications of colonialism and its political legacies.

Presenting works in unconventional places and not simply on the white walls of the gallery or museum, André Eugène employs a variety of found materials to challenge authority and class hierarchies as they are played out in Haiti's sociocultural system. Visually inscribed in his use of discarded materials are the transformative possibilities of a *second life* for such objects, asking what they can offer us as part of contemporary artistic practices. He blurs the line between artist and community member as his dynamic works boldly occupy the urban artists' camps of Port-au-Prince's Grand Rue and transform pristine gallery spaces in Haiti and abroad.

Eugène is one of the founding members of the group of Haitian sculptors of Grand Rue, Atis Rezistans, along with Frantz Jacques (Guyodo) and Jean Hérard Celeur.[9] Writing about Atis Rezistans, Leah Gordon states,

> the work of these three artists is a varying hybrid of classic woodcarving, metal sculpture and assemblage. Their muscular sculptural collages of engine manifolds, computer entrails, TV sets, medical debris, skulls and discarded timber transform the detritus of a failing economy into deranged, post-apocalyptic totems.[10]

In his figurative sculpture *Ayiti Pap Peri* (cat. no. 11), Eugène alludes to the strength of the Haitian people who survived and continue to survive the deadly earthquake of January 12, 2010 that resulted in the death of over 300,000 people. A compilation of scraps of wood, plastic, tires, rubber, metal, and sundry other materials, *Ayiti Pap Peri* symbolizes the "transformative act of assemblage."[11] Eugène is aesthetically methodical and creatively systematic in the formal placement of wood, plastic, and metal, paying close attention to the balance of materials in this sculptural assemblage. The tire rim metal frame that forms Erzulie's halo is balanced by repurposed rubber that transforms into a protective shield and warm cocoon for the baby Jesus. Several interlacing nails create the recognizable scar on the face of the fearlessly loyal and protective Erzulie Dantor/Ezili Dantò, the patron *lwa* of women, mothers, and children. He continues the tradition of wood sculpture that was perfected by Nacius Joseph (cat. no. 16) and Jean Camille Nasson, whose carved wooden figures are adorned with all forms of discarded materials. In addition, his use of assemblage shares the same sensibilities of the work of African American artists Noah Purifoy, Betye Saar, and John Outterbridge whose artful engagement with found objects and repurposed materials express social and political commentary. Like their works, Eugène's pieces maintain a political consciousness while interweaving visual poetics strongly grounded in vernacular aesthetic practices. In dynamic creative approaches and with deep clarity, they employ what Donald J. Cosentino calls a "black Atlantic aesthetic of assemblage."[12] What Eugène brings to this tradition is a certain playfulness that evocatively blends the political with the erotic, and the social with the sacred. His ability to transform mundane, discarded material into beautiful sculptures speaks to his understanding of form, style, and aesthetics. In their formal rigor, his sculptures narrate the tensions surrounding power and history, social class and color, the disenfranchised and the disempowered, dilemmas that have plagued the black diaspora. His bringing together of disparate objects, combining imagery that underscores the ironies of imperialism and the hierarchies of class, is what makes Eugène an engaging and provocative artist.

Furthermore, what is most exciting about Eugène is his advancement of the imaginative aesthetic possibilities of the art collective. Art collectives have been a vibrant and fruitful part of black Atlantic artistic communities. In 1963, for example, painters Romare Bearden, Norman Lewis, and Hale Woodruff organized Spiral, a collective of African American artists with Emma Amos later joining their ranks. AfriCobra, started in 1968 in Chicago, was founded by African American artists Jeff Donaldson, Wadsworth Jarrell, Gerald Williams, and Barbara Jones-Hogu. In Haiti, the Saint-Soleil collective was founded in the early 1970s by Maud Robard and Tiga (Jean-Claude Garoute) and later joined by Levoy Exil (cat. no. 12), Prosper Pierre-Louis (cat. nos. 21 and 22), and Louisiane Saint Fleurant (cat. no. 23). Today, the members of the well-known Cuban art collective Los Carpinteros create drawings, sculptures, installations, and site-specific works that artfully blend biting humor and irony with covert political significance. As a collective, Atis Rezistans has acquired a "bohemian swagger" allowing it to critique the oppressive "*boujzwa* norms" that have created the dilapidated and abandoned factories that now provide materials for their artwork.[13] Eugène's aesthetic practice is rooted in the materials and realities of urban life and urban decay, neighborhoods that exist in the marginalized spaces of downtown Port-au-Prince. His work manifests a sophisticated negotiation of post-modernity that comes of living in communities on the margins of society surrounded by debris and discarded materials yet where an underlying vitality and resistance is embedded in the creative process and production that can potentially transform urban spaces.

An established multi-disciplinary artist, Mario Benjamin has exhibited extensively in galleries and at numerous biennials, creating site-specific installations that are prophetic and evocative interactions with color, form, light, and space. *Untitled* (cat. no. 4), from 1996, is a classic Benjamin painting, employing mixed-media and deep rich colors to create this dual portrait. On the left side of the painting, a full frontal view of a man is rendered in a realistic fashion using dark lines to underscore his pensive, enigmatic stare. On the right is another image of a man, whose melancholy features and air of mystery are compounded by the faint line drawing. It seems as if Benjamin first traced the image on the right and later decided that the left side worked much better. The bottom part of the painting uses broad brushstrokes in muted browns and beiges to create a startling abstract contrast to the deep reds that decorate the top part of the painting. The images are placed side by side, center stage within the pictorial space, attracting the contemplative gaze of the viewer. The interplay of emotions is always bubbling beneath the surface of Benjamin's work. Well-known for his brooding images with dark colors, Benjamin's *Untitled* does not disappoint. The slightly thicker application of paint layered onto the Masonite gives the features on the left side of this dual portrait a great sense of emotive depth. Through the affective power of color, the anguish of the sitter is conveyed and we wonder perhaps at the conundrum that gives his eyes that circumspect expression. The work evokes more meaning than a mere engagement with paint and texture. It is the frenzied yet controlled style that suggests an intensive expressiveness and an immediate encounter with the grittiness of the Masonite. Its textured appearance lends itself well to the scratches and marks purposely etched onto the surface.

Benjamin works abstractly with form and figure. The adroit brushwork and dark and intense colors of the painting express an almost nihilistic energy and charisma. He is a consummate colorist, employing the characteristics of Abstract Expressionism and German Expressionism in his use of hue and formal distortion to evoke meaning and emotions. The techniques in Benjamin's work are also present in the paintings of Sacha Tebó, albeit executed differently. In both *Le Mariage* and *Portrait of a Man* (cat. nos. 24 and 25), Tebó applies large brushstrokes in greens and yellows to create a dialogue between color and abstract form. His wedding portrait, *Le Mariage*, depicts a happy occasion as illustrated by the pale and calming hues of blues, oranges, and whites, while the greens, reds, and oranges used in *Portrait of a Man* evoke the serious anxiety of a lone man crouched and clutching at his head. Tebó's application of wax on the canvases coupled with his use of subtle and muted colors give the works a greater sense of depth and texture, also signaled by the grooved abstract outlines of the figures. Benjamin's and Tebó's affecting use of color is reminiscent of the miniature diptych *Toussaint et George* (2010) by Trinidadian artist Nikolai Noel (illustration 6). Noel's piece depicts the "father of the republic of Haiti," Toussaint L'Ouverture, and the "father of the United States of America," George Washington.[14] In classic portraiture style, a thin gray wash, light graphite, and linseed oil compose Washington's frontal image. His "lightness" is sharply juxtaposed against Toussaint's facial features, which are thickly outlined in black acrylic paint. The deliberately ridged and grooved surface of

Illustration 6

Nikolai Noel
Toussaint et George, 2010
Acrylic, graphite and linseed oil
on panel
10 x 8 in.
© 2010 Nikolai Noel

the panel suggests a coarse unevenness to the piece and adds a vintage element to the painting. The black acrylic paint gives Toussaint a "gruesome mask-like appearance" making him, through his darkness, impenetrable while the "father of the United States of America," remains translucent in his light gray wash.[15] It is as if the texture of the paint has affixed itself onto the texture of the flesh, ascribing incomprehensibility to one image and decipherability to the other.

A visual representation of the subject is what portraiture seeks to communicate, often through the use of symbols and materials, as well as through the artist's own formal and stylistic approaches. What is clear is that through portraiture, the face is the site where identity is legible and history can be read. Perhaps Noel's goal, like Benjamin's, is not to use the skin as an impervious barrier that seals the body from the world, but to make visible the global impact that skin has had on history, and history has had on skin. Noel has not saturated the canvas with paint; instead Haiti's historicity is evoked through the use and contrast of light and dark colors and the heavy and thinly applied paint. While Noel's work is monochromatic, Benjamin offers us a burst of sober colors. Possibly what Benjamin gives us through his paintings, and most recently his light-based and sound installation projects, is hope for the livability of Haiti even in its more difficult and troubling moments.

I close this essay with several recommendations: first to explore further the ways in which artists of Haitian descent are part of diasporic and transnational fields of artistic and imaginative inquiry. Second, I encourage those who write about and document modern and contemporary diasporic Haitian art and visual cultural practices to broaden what is understood as "Haitian art" to include creative projects that articulate multi-dimensional and multivalent artistic practices, thereby removing this designation from the modernist "primitivist" rhetoric propagated by sensationalist works of fiction, film, and theater during the 1920s, 1930s, and 1940s. Such projects would explore parallel dialogues and tease out the shared or possibly conflicting imaginative engagements among individuals such as multimedia artist Maxence

(Maksaens) Denis and Mario Benjamin; mixed-media artist Adler Guerrier and Edouard Duval-Carrié; performance artist Gina Athena Ulysse and Frantz Zéphirin (cat. no. 28); performance artist and poet Lenelle Moïse and André Eugène; performance artist and poet Gabrielle Civil and Myrlande Constant; and film maker Kervans Barthelemy and Pascale Monnin. Such projects would provide us with the ability, as Kobena Mercer contends, to "comprehend the transnational networks of artistic connections."[16] What I hope for is a conversation about Haitian art that is not framed simply within the fields of religion and politics but is rather situated within a discourse that gives primacy and critical depth to its vibrant and syncretic aesthetic and art histories. It is then that we can move away from the limited interpretations of symbols and images that typify artwork that has come to be identified as "Haitian art." Such a shift will enable us to explore the ways in which works of art produced in Haiti and in the diaspora can be discussed with reference to national and global aesthetic practices and within comparative art histories, refuting, as Trouillot suggests, the "fiction of Haitian exceptionalism."

***

[1] Michel-Rolph Trouillot, "The Odd and the Ordinary: Haiti, the Caribbean, and the World," *Cimarrón: New Perspectives on the Caribbean* 2, no. 3 (Winter 1990): 11.

[2] DeWitt Peters, "Haiti's Primitive Painters," *Harper's Bazaar* (January 1947): 104.

[3] Trouillot, "The Odd and the Ordinary: Haiti, the Caribbean, and the World," 6.

[4] Trouillot, "The Odd and the Ordinary: Haiti, the Caribbean, and the World," 3. Trouillot takes this passage from what he calls "a sensationalist account of Haitian history written by Marine Colonel Robert Heinl and his wife Nancy." Robert Debs Heinl and Nancy Gordon Heinl, *Written in Blood: The Story of the Haitian People, 1492-1995* (Maryland: University Press of America, 1978), 1.

[5] "Ebony G. Patterson," *National Gallery of Jamaica Blog*, January 6, 2010, web.

[6] Pascale Monnin, Skyped interview by author, July 9, 2014.

[7] Artist's website.

[8] Florine Demosthene, interview by author, October 25, 2013, Brooklyn, New York.

[9] Katherine Smith writes that Guyodo left the collective in 2009 but still works in the neighborhood. See Smith, "Genealogies of Gede," in *In Extremis: Death and Life in 21st-Century Haitian Art*, ed. Donald J. Cosentino (Los Angeles: Fowler Museum of Art, 2012), 85-99.

[10] Leah Gordon, "The Sculptors of Grand Rue," *Raw Vision* 65 (Winter 2008/2009), n.p.

[11] "Atis Rezistans: The Story of the Grand Rue Sculptors," web.

[12] Donald J. Cosentino, "Baby on the Blender: A Visual History of Catastrophe in Haiti," *Small Axe* 15, no. 36 (2011): 142.

[13] Cosentino, "Baby on the Blender: A Visual History of Catastrophe in Haiti," *Small Axe* 15, no. 36 (2011): 150.

[14] Noel's piece was shown in 2011 in *Wrestling with the Image: Caribbean Interventions*, an exhibition featuring the artwork of contemporary artists from twelve Caribbean countries at the Art Museum of the Americas, Washington, D.C.

[15] Tatiana Flores, "In Defense of Palm Trees," in *Wrestling with the Image: Caribbean Interventions*, exhibition e-catalogue, eds. Christopher Cozier and Tatiana Flores (2011), n.p., web.

[16] Kobena Mercer, "Cosmopolitan Contact Zones," in *Afro-Modern: Journeys Through the Black Atlantic*, eds. Tanya Barson and Peter Gorschlüter (Liverpool: Tate Liverpool, 2010), 40. In this provocative essay, Mercer identifies Haiti as an important "cosmopolitan contact zone" for the cross-cultural artistic dialogues that contribute to the making of an Afro-Modernism, bringing together U.S. American, European, and Spanish Caribbean visual artists with Haitian visual artists. The following is a selected list of equally useful materials that explore these transnational connections:

James Porter, "'Picturesque Haiti,'" *Opportunity* 24, no. 4 (October–December 1946): 178–79; Philippe Thoby-Marcelin, *Art in Latin America Today: Haiti* (Washington, D.C.: Pan American Union, 1959); Krista Thompson, "Preoccupied with Haiti: The Dream of Diaspora in African American Art, 1915-1942," *American Art Journal* (Fall 2007): 75-97; Margaret Rose Vendryes, "Brothers Under the Skin: Richmond Barthé in Haiti," *Journal of Haitian Studies* 10, no. 2 (Fall 2004): 116-134; Harriet G. Warkel, "Image and Identity: The Art of William E. Scott, John W. Hardrick, and Hale A. Woodruff," in *A Shared Heritage: Art by Four African Americans*, eds. William E. Taylor and Harriet G. Warkel (Indianapolis: Indianapolis Museum of Art and Indiana University Press, 1996), 17-76.

CATALOGUE ENTRIES / WORKS IN THE EXHIBITION

1

Gesner Abelard
b. 1922, Port-au-Prince, Haiti
Birds and Foliage, ca. 1960
oil on masonite
15 1/2 x 23 3/8 in. (39.4 x 59.4 cm)
Gift of the Estate of Dr. Edward J. Carroll, 2001.21.30

After working as a mechanic, Gesner Abelard began studying painting and sculpture at the Industrial School of Port-au-Prince. It was around that time, in 1946, that the then-director of the Centre d'Art DeWitt Peters took notice of Abelard's talent and invited him to join this recently founded creative center. At the Centre d'Art Abelard gained access to materials and received mentorship from the other artists based there. He quickly developed a unique point of view while working in the style labeled "naïve." In *Birds and Foliage*, Abelard depicts his subject matter of choice. A multitude of colorful birds perched atop branches of foliage dominate the scene, a technique characteristically seen throughout his oeuvre. By interspersing vibrantly hued birds among flowering branches, Abelard forces the viewer to stop and search for each individual bird. Through his use of detail, Gesner Abelard succeeds in transforming a simple theme into a complex composition.

- Katherine Mato

2

Clotaire Bazile
b. 1946, Haiti
d. 2012, Haiti
Drapo Vodou: Erzulie Freda and Dambala Ouedo, ca. 1974
satin, glass beads, plastic beads, sequins, and printed image
38 5/8 x 34 in. (98.1 x 86.4 cm)
Gift of Marvin Ross Friedman and Adrienne bon Haes in honor of Kimberly Green, 2011.18
© Clotaire Bazile

3

Clotaire Bazile
b. 1946, Haiti
d. 2012, Haiti
Drapo Vodou: Saint Jacques Majeur, ca. 2012
satin, sequins, beads, printed images, and plastic
39 1/2 × 36 in. (100.3 × 91.4 cm)
Gift of Brian A. Dursum in memory of Michael J. McEachen, 2013.12
© Clotaire Bazile

Among Vodouyizan (practitioners of Vodou), the *drapo* (flag) is one of the most sacred objects, serving as a temporal greeting to the *lwa* (spirit) during a *sèvis* (ceremony). The *drapo* has also become one of the most recognized contemporary Haitian art pieces thanks in part to the work of Clotaire Bazile, an *oungan* (priest) and one of the great contemporary Vodou flagmakers. He had no formal training when he created his first *drapo* in the early 1970s, which he said was based on a vision he received from a *lwa*. The aesthetic and commercial interest in his *drapo* came in 1973 when two French tourists saw his work. Bazile's *drapo* illustrate common elements seen in both *drapo sèvis* and art *drapo*: the central design, often the *vèvè* (cosmogram) associated with the *lwa* or an image of the Catholic saint identified with that spirit; the background or field; and a border. Bazile's style is characterized by an emphasis on geometric forms, especially in the borders, and vibrant colors. His work exhibits a high level of craftsmanship: the sequins overlap precisely, they are sewn on tightly, and all lines are straight.

Erzulie Freda, Dambala and Ayida Ouedo, and Saint Jacques Majeur, four of the most beloved and important *lwa* in Haitian Vodou, are featured on Clotaire Bazile's flags. Erzulie Freda, the *lwa* of love, is often shown with Dambala and Ayida on *drapo*. This composition, a heart framed by two snakes, is Bazile's earliest motif. Dambala and Ayida embody the principles of birth and creation — an idea reinforced by the eggs over the central design. The predominant pink color is associated with Erzulie Freda, and the overall pastel shades indicate that these are "cool" spirits, sources of wisdom and comfort. In contrast, Saint Jacques Majeur, a Catholic saint recognized as the *lwa* Ogou, is a "hot" spirit as the dominant red signifies. Ogou, identified with the Haitian Revolution's struggle against slavery and colonialism, symbolizes power. The relationship between Vodou and Roman Catholicism is also evident in the *drapo* honoring Erzulie Freda, which features an image from the Catholic chromolithograph of the Virgin Mary as Mater Dolorosa. These *drapo* illustrate Bazile's development as an artist: the flag dedicated to Erzulie Freda and Dambala Ouedo, one of his earliest commercial *drapo*, has a simple border, while that honoring Saint Jacques, one of the last he created before his tragic disappearance in 2012, has a more intricate border.

- M. Stephanie Chancy

4

Mario Benjamin
b. 1964, Port-au-Prince, Haiti
Untitled, ca. 1996
mixed media on masonite
60 x 48 1/4 x 3 7/8 in. (152.4 x 122.6 x 9.8 cm)
Gift of Dr. and Mrs. Carl Eisdorfer, 2002.57.48

After Mario Benjamin abandoned an early career as a photo-realist painter he continued to explore portraiture in experimental modes. In this work, he paints what appears to be a double portrait of two men floating within an open-book-like structure, one who has strong features and the other whose countenance is less distinct and partially obscured. The portraits are oriented at a three-quarter view, both men staring toward their right. The upper portion of the painting is bright red, while the lower half contains various shades of brown, and appears to have scratches throughout. Benjamin notes of his process, "I begin with a formal sketch, I deconstruct it until it is destroyed… and then it appears…within the light." In recent years Benjamin has become well-known for multimedia installations that transform space with sculpture, found objects, lighting, video, and sound.

\- Katherine Mato and Kate Ramsey

5

Jean Charlemagne
b. 1950, Haiti
Domino Players, 1988
acrylic on canvas
19 5/8 x 15 5/8 in. (49.8 x 39.7 cm)
Museum purchase through funds from Brian A. Dursum, 2005.9

Jean Charlemagne moved to New York in the 1970s to pursue his dream of becoming an artist. Eventually he began showcasing his work at small galleries, receiving recognition as one of Haiti's emerging contemporary artists. His work encompasses many of the elements for which Haitian art is celebrated, including themes of quotidian life and elements from the so-called "naïve" style of painting. In *Domino Players*, painted after his move to New York, Charlemagne depicts leisure activities commonly played in his home county. In the foreground two boys kneel, playing marbles. Behind them sit three men playing dominoes, who are the focus of this work. The two figures on either side of the table appear to be immersed in the game, while the man in the center stares directly forward, as if questioning why the viewer is watching. Behind them is the Haitian countryside, full of thatched roof homes and green mountains. Charlemagne creates a painting that resonates broadly by centering this work on games found throughout the world, as well as by including an element commonly seen in western painting — a hierarchical structure.

- Katherine Mato

6

Jean René Chery
b. 1928, Haiti
Skipping Rope, not dated
acrylic on masonite
11 3/4 x 15 3/4 in. (29.8 x 40 cm)
Gift of Richard Levine, 84.0175

Known for his paintings of rural scenes and regional peoples, Jean René Chery's *Skipping Rope* is representative of the artist's oeuvre. Depicted are eight young girls skipping rope before a landscaped high white wall.

The latter may enclose the grounds of an institution or of a large private home. The girls are clothed in bright dresses with bows in their hair, possibly indicating that this scene takes place on a school day or after church services. This work by Chery falls into the genre of Haitian painting focused on children's activities, such as play or chores. In capturing a magical moment when at least five of the girls are aloft, Chery's painting evokes the rhythm, focus, and buoyancy of childhood games.

- Katherine Mato and Kate Ramsey

7 Before becoming a flagmaker, Myrlande Constant worked as a seamstress in a wedding dress factory where she learned the technique of beaded embroidery. Her distinctive skillset has enabled her to become one of the most innovative contemporary *drapo vodou* (Vodou flag) artists working today. Constant uses a crochet hook rather than a needle to create her designs and works with the back of the piece facing her. In *Points Saint Miel*, she combines sequins with beadwork to create a flag rich in detail and nuance. According to Constant, the Saint Miel are a diverse group of spirits originating in both the Petwo and Rada traditions of Vodou who shape all aspects of life in the community they populate. The narrative of this flag centers on scenes of life and death around the *mapou*, a tree of life, sacred in Vodou. Life is depicted on the left where a woman is giving birth; at the center, a mortuary preparation is portrayed; and on the right, a gravesite is figured with Gede *lwa* congregating around the black cross symbolizing Bawon Samdi, who oversees the Gede spirits and cemeteries. A banner featuring the colors of the Haitian flag is planted nearby. Angels, representing Catholic saints and Vodou spirits, float above the scene, one of them reaching down as if trying to lift up the dead. In the background is the Haitian countryside, where spiritual and everyday worlds are closely interconnected.

- Katherine Mato and Louis Herns Marcelin

Myrlande Constant
b. 1968, Port-au-Prince, Haiti
Points Saint Miel, 2005
Sequins and beads on cloth
51 x 48 in (129.5 x 121.9 cm)
Museum purchase, 2014.14
© 2005 Myrlande Constant

8

Florine Demosthene
b. New York City, United States
Assed Out from *The Capture Series,* 2010
ink, charcoal, graphite and oil bar on polypropylene
13 1/8 × 10 3/4 in. (33.3 × 27.3 cm)
Museum purchase, 2014.1
© 2010 Florine Demosthene

Florine Demosthene moved from Haiti to New York as a young adult and earned her BFA from Parsons The New School for Design and her MFA from Hunter College. Since then, her work has been shown in exhibitions in the United States, the Caribbean, Africa, and Europe. Demosthene's recent work examines constructions of race, gender, and sexuality by exploring and exploding stereotypes of the black female body within contemporary visual culture. Demosthene notes that her series *The Capture* is "an attempt to structure a new mythology that explores black female sexuality and sensuality" by "delving into the subconscious mind of a fictitious black heroine and the ephemeral quality of her thoughts and experiences." This set of works has been inspired and shaped by Demosthene's travels in West Africa, Haiti, and other parts of the Caribbean. In *Assed Out* from *The Capture Series,*

Demosthene's heroine towers above a rubble-strewn and crumbling landscape, her solidity seeming to stabilize a disorienting physical world that appears still in motion. The title is a colloquialism with multiple meanings, including extremely tired and out of luck.

- Katherine Mato and Kate Ramsey

9

Préfète Duffaut
b. 1923, Cyvadier, Haiti
d. 2012, Port-au-Prince, Haiti
Troisième tentation (Third Temptation), ca. 1965
oil on canvas
50 5/8 x 83 3/8 in. (128.6 x 211.8 cm)
Museum purchase through funds from Jewel Schainack Stein, 70.005.000
© Préfète Duffaut

Préfète Duffaut's *Troisième Tentation* depicts the third temptation of Jesus Christ. In the biblical account of this trial, Satan takes Christ to the highest mountaintop from where all the earthly kingdoms can be seen and tells Christ that if he worships him, all will be his. Christ must then choose between good and evil, and it is this critical moment within the third temptation that is represented in this work. Duffaut sets this scene in and above an imaginary city featuring Catholic and Vodou iconography. Urban and mountainous locales are interconnected through a network of crisscrossing roads and footpaths that lead to different realms presided over by brilliantly figured spiritual beings. Seaside cities similar to this are seen throughout Duffaut's oeuvre, inspired by the artist's hometown of Jacmel in the south of Haiti. Like many of his contemporaries, Duffaut spent considerable time at the Centre d'Art in Port-au-Prince. He went on to become one of Haiti's most prominent artists, and was one of several invited to paint murals in Port-au-Prince's Cathédrale Sainte Trinité, largely destroyed by the January 12, 2010 earthquake.

- Katherine Mato and Louis Herns Marcelin

10

Edouard Duval-Carrié
b. 1954, Port-au-Prince, Haiti
Trois feuilles (Three Leaves), ca. 1998
mixed media and artist-made frame
73 1/4 x 82 in. (186.1 x 208.3 cm)
Gift of Marilyn Holifield and Marvin Holloway, 2002.45
© 1998 Edouard Duval-Carrié

Born in Port-au-Prince, Edouard Duval-Carrié spent much of his childhood with his family in Puerto Rico, in exile from the François Duvalier regime. He then lived in Canada and France, before settling in Miami in the early 1990s. Influenced by this migratory experience, Duval-Carrié's paintings, sculptures, and installations re-envision the history, politics, and culture of Haiti through surrealist bricolage. Creating his multimedia works by assembling bits and pieces of disparate, yet interconnected, materials — a process he has described as "chronicling" — Duval-Carrié reconstructs, reinterprets, and transforms received narratives of Haiti's past and present.

In the form of a classic altarpiece, Duval-Carrié's *Trois Feuilles* thematizes the centrality of religion in Haitian society. The title, meaning "three leaves," is drawn from a Vodou ritual song that reflects on exile, survival, and remembrance. Duval-Carrié alludes to the Christian iconography of the holy trinity in his brilliant reimagining of three Vodou *lwa* (spirits) juxtaposed against a fecund tropical paradise reminiscent of both Eden and mythic Africa. *Trois Feuilles* highlights the interconnection between the natural and the spiritual worlds, invoking the belief that herbs and leaves are powerful tools when working with the spirits. This tableau is surrounded by other niche cuts in the surface of the work, featuring gold-colored palm trees, icons, and what appear to be bullet encasings. In this as in his other works, Duval-Carrié ruminates on how trauma and dislocation can both obliterate and incite memory, and how the process of reconstruction can also be a practice of healing.

- Jennifer Garcon

11

André Eugène
b. 1959, Port-au-Prince, Haiti
Ayiti Pap Peri (Haiti Will Not Perish), 2013
wood, plastic, tires and metal
43 × 21 × 13 in. (109.2 × 53.3 × 33 cm)
Museum purchase, 2014.2
© 2013 André Eugène

André Eugène is a member of the Sculptors of the Grand Rue, also known as Atis Rezistans, a collective of contemporary Haitian artists who live and work in a community at the southern end of the main avenue that runs through downtown Port-au-Prince. Along with his colleagues, Eugène has been hosting Haiti's Ghetto Biennale, an art exhibition designed to reveal social, racial, class, and geographical immobilities, since 2009. In *Ayiti Pap Peri*, Eugène created a powerful sculpture out of a variety of found objects, including tires, driftwood, and metal. The title of the work, which translates to *Haiti Will Not Perish*, may be a reference to the artist's home country after the 2010 earthquake. The sculpture depicts a mother with her child, possibly evoking the *lwa* Ezili Dantò, who is a powerful single mother typically depicted with facial scars. Similar to German artist Kurt Schwitters' *Merz Column*, created in 1923 and destroyed by bombs during World

War II, *Ayiti Pap Peri* begins with abstracted objects at its base and slowly becomes more figurative, eventually leading up to a human-like head with a surrounding halo. Eugène's likely references to artists like Schwitters and Marcel Duchamp, with his use of the readymade, allows this sculpture to resonate with a multitude of viewers, evoking a remembrance of Haiti's strength.

- Katherine Mato

12

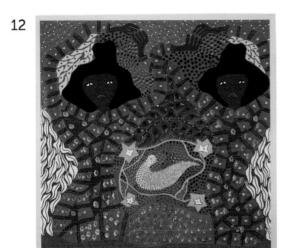

Levoy Exil
b. 1944, Fermathe, Haiti
Untitled, 1988
acrylic on masonite
23 5/8 x 23 5/8 in. (60 x 60 cm)
Gift of Anne Doniger, 2002.41.2

Levoy Exil was one of the founding members of the Saint-Soleil (Holy Sun) art movement that was initiated by artist Jean-Claude Garoute (Tiga) and Maud Robard in the rural community of Soisson-la-Montagne in 1972. Aiming to explore popular aesthetics outside of the commercialization of the art market, the collective provided fine art materials to local residents, who also extracted their own dyes from plants and seeds. Levoy Exil became one of the most prominent

Saint-Soleil artists and went on to form the Cinq Soleils (Five Suns) group with four others, including Prosper Pierre-Louis and Louisiane Saint Fleurant. Like the work of other Saint-Soleil artists, many of Exil's paintings have a mystical quality and feature abstracted images of Vodou *lwa*. In this *Untitled* work, two seemingly identical female figures appear on either side, staring directly toward the viewer, their undulating arms encircling their heads. Exil is likely depicting the *lwa marasa*, or divine twins, who were a frequent subject of his work, and here appear so connected that they merge with one another, enclosing a white dove between them.

- Katherine Mato and Kate Ramsey

13

Alexandre Grégoire
b. 1922, Jacmel, Haiti
d. 2001, Jacmel, Haiti
Madonna and Child with Altars to Lwa, not dated
oil on masonite
15 3/8 x 23 1/2 in. (39.1 x 59.7 cm)
Gift of Gonzalo and Louise Valdes-Fauli, 2000.021.05

In 1968, with the support of the Centre d'Art in Port-au-Prince, Alexandre Grégoire ended his career as a band member at the National

Palace and began painting. Common themes depicted in his oeuvre include religion, quotidian life in Haiti, and historical events, most of which were painted in the so-called "naïve" style. In Grégoire's *Madonna and Child with Altars to Lwa*, the artist depicts the interconnection of Roman Catholicism and Vodou. In the center are patterned steps leading up to the Madonna holding the child on her left arm. Grégoire may have chosen to portray them with dark skin in reference to Notre Dame du Perpétual Secours who is Haiti's patron saint. On either side of the figures are tables with offerings to *lwa*. In the background stand several flowers in a variety of colors, mirroring those found in the peacocks placed at the entrance of the steps.

- Katherine Mato and Louis Herns Marcelin

14

Voltaire Hector
b. 1952, Port-au-Prince, Haiti
Manbo a ap fe apel a Erzulie Freda li ap vini (The Manbo Is Calling Erzulie Freda; She Is Coming), not dated
oil on canvas
19 3/8 x 23 5/8 in. (49.2 x 60 cm)
Museum purchase through funds from Brian A. Dursum, 2002.31.1

Voltaire Hector began painting in 1977 with the encouragement of his brother, Roland Hector. Hector initially painted simple landscapes, and it was not until his brother's death that he broadened his narrative depictions to include scenes of family life, religious ceremonies, healing practices, Haitian politics, and autobiographical events, among other themes. As seen in many of Hector's works, the title of the painting is written in the lower-left corner. In the foreground kneels the *manbo,* or female priest, as she calls upon Erzulie Freda, the spirit of love and beauty. The *manbo* draws the *vèvè* (ritual design) associated with Erzulie Freda in order to invite her, as the *lwa* arrives in the background clothed in shades of blue, red, and white. A lush landscape is visible behind these figures, embedded surrealistically with wide-open eyes and a door frame leading to another ritual space.

- Katherine Mato

15 Serge Jolimeau is part of a long tradition of metal sculptors from the town of Croix-des-Bouquets. His artistic lineage can be traced back to the father of Haitian sculptors, Georges Liautaud, a blacksmith first known for creating cemetery crosses. Jolimeau studied with Seresier Louisjuste, one of Liautaud's disciples and a distinguished artist in his own right. Jolimeau is one of the best-known Haitian metal sculptors working today. Like his predecessors, he uses recycled oil drums that are cleaned, fired, and flattened into rectangles. The design is drawn and then carefully cut out. Jolimeau's work is recognized for its elegance, its emphasis on the sensuous curved line, and its radiating warmth. *La Sirène* exemplifies these characteristics. The circular motif is accentuated in the overall composition and reinforced by the details along the mermaid's fins and hair. These elements, which were added using the technique of *repoussé* (pounded or pushed out from the back) add texture to the piece. As the marine personification of the *lwa* Ezili Freda, *La Sirène* bestows wealth and beauty on those who serve her.

- M. Stephanie Chancy

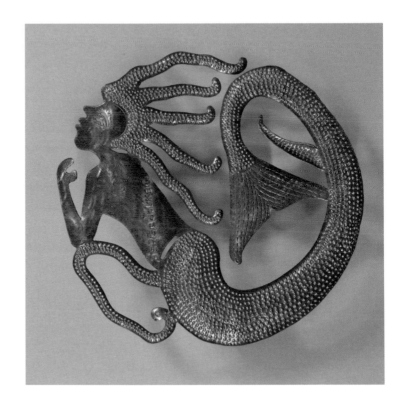

Serge Jolimeau
b. 1952, Croix des Bouquets, Haiti
La Sirène (The Mermaid), ca. 1980
varnished steel
1/4 x 10 1/4 in. (0.6 x 26 cm)
Museum purchase through funds from
Brian A. Dursum, 98.0020.03
© 1980 Serge Jolimeau

16

Nacius Joseph
b. 1939, Petit-Goâve, Haiti
Boat People, ca. 1982
wood
10 x 39 x 1 1/4 in. (25.4 x 99.1 x 3.2 cm)
Gift of Dr. and Mrs. Bernard M. Wagner, 99.0014.03

Nacius Joseph began his artistic career working alongside sculptor Gilbert Duperrier in Port-au-Prince, but truly defined his artistic style after returning to his hometown of Petit-Goâve. Eventually becoming Haiti's first internationally recognized wood sculptor, Joseph owes some of the popularity of his work to Pierre Monosiet, Haitian painter and former director of the Musée d'Art Haïtien, and author Selden Rodman, who refers to him as a "Sculptor of Genius."

Joseph created *Boat People* in the context of an increasing surge of Haitian migrants making the perilous journey to the United States and other parts of the Caribbean by sea, fleeing a reality torn apart by economic and political devastation. In September 1981, Jean-Claude Duvalier signed an interdiction and repatriation agreement with the Reagan administration to stem the tide of migrants heading to U.S. shores. In this sculpture, the passengers seem to look ahead with the hope that they will survive their voyage and find better opportunities than those available in their homeland. The central figure holds a fish that might represent the image of Saint Ulrich, the Catholic saint associated with Agwe, the *lwa* of the sea, who would protect them during their passage.

- Hadassah St. Hubert

17

Gabriel Lévêque
b. 1923, Croix-des-Bouquets, Haiti
Five Angels with Musical Instruments, not dated
acrylic on masonite
15 5/8 x 23 3/4 in. (39.7 x 60.3 cm)
Gift of Richard Levine, 84.0178

Gabriel Lévêque was among the first generation of artists associated with the Centre d'Art, founded in 1944, and was one of those commissioned to paint the murals above the altar in Port-au-Prince's Cathédrale Sainte Trinité. Lévêque contributed three panels in the upper reaches of the apse, depicting angels heralding with horns and bearing garlands. Most of the Sainte Trinité murals, which portrayed biblical scenes featuring figures of African descent, were destroyed in the 2010 earthquake. Lévêque's *Five Angels with Musical Instruments* reflects his iconographic style and returns to the religious figures who are a frequent theme of his work. In the foreground sit five angels dressed in blue playing wind and string instruments. In the background myriad colorful flowers converge to create a vaulting arch behind the angels, as well as an implied halo above the central figure.

- Katherine Mato and Kate Ramsey

18   **Joseph Louisjuste**
b. ?, Croix-des-Bouquets, Haiti
Screen, not dated
iron
76 1/4 x 57 x 3/4 in. (193.7 x 144.8 x 1.9 cm)
Bequest of Larue Storm, 2006.27.21

Joseph Louisjuste was born in Croix-des-Bouquets, a town in Haiti famous for its metal workshops. Along with his two brothers, Seresier and Janvier, he learned the art of metalwork from Georges Liautaud, who was the first metal artist to create sculptures for the art market. The three Louisjuste brothers would later go on to be prominent pioneers of Haitian metalwork, teaching the next generation of metal artists in their hometown. Like many pieces by Haitian artists who work in metal, most of Louisjuste's sculptures are small in scale and likely to be hung on walls. His *Screen*, however, is a large-scale sculptural work of art that is meant to stand on its own. Originating in ancient China, screens are commonly intended to be decorative pieces that serve as dividers between spaces, and to increase privacy. Given that Louisjuste's *Screen* has cutouts throughout, creating intricate patterns resembling human and snake-like figures, its purpose as a means of privacy is reduced. Louisjuste thus calls attention to the *Screen's* artistic metalwork and succeeds in transforming what might otherwise be considered a functional or decorative piece into a work of art.

- Katherine Mato

19 **Seresier Louisjuste**
b. ?, Croix-des-Bouquets, Haiti
Danbala Wedo, not dated
iron
68 x 8 in. (172.7 x 20.3 cm)
Bequest of Larue Storm, 2006.27.22

Like his brother Joseph Louisjuste, whose work is also displayed in this exhibition, Seresier Louisjuste was born in Croix-des-Bouquets and specializes in sculptures created in metal. Many of his works include narratives associated with the Vodou religion. In *Danbala Wedo,* Louisjuste creates an iron wall sculpture rendering one of the most august and important *lwa,* Danbala Wedo. This ancient *lwa* is closely associated with the creation of life, rainbows, and serpents — hence the figure Louisjuste sculpts in his *Danbala Wedo.* The technique used to create the different forms within the sculpture is reminiscent of that used by French modernist Henri Matisse in his cutouts. By employing his own version of the cutout technique, the artist is able to explore positive and negative space, allowing the latter to become part of the work. *Danbala Wedo* is long and narrow in shape, with the central figure pointing up towards the heavens. The serpent-like figure that constitutes almost the entirety of this sculpture morphs into a human-like head upon reaching the upper edge of its body. On either side of the snake-like form are abstract patterns resembling a myriad of plants and animals. The abstract figures are secondary to the representation of the *lwa,* which reminds the viewer of Danbala Wedo's significance.

- Katherine Mato

20

Pascale Monnin
b. 1974, Port-au-Prince, Haiti
L'Ange de la Résurrection (Resurrection Angel), 2006-2011
pottery with raku glaze, wire, pearls, and jewels
60 x 24 x 20 in. (150 x 60 x 50 cm)
Generous gift of Beaux Arts in honor of retiring Director Brian A. Dursum, 2014.13
© 2006-2011 Pascale Monnin

Pascale Monnin moved from Haiti to Switzerland at a young age but each year traveled back to Haiti where her family ran a prominent gallery. Monnin's arts education took place in both locations, and at age twenty she decided to settle permanently in Haiti. In *L'Ange de la Résurrection*, begun in 2006 and completed in 2011, Monnin speaks to the indestructible spirit of the Haitian people. In a statement she released about this work, she notes, "It is the face of a child split by a diamond-studded fault line. The face teaches us the need to live with our scars, to make our stitches sparkling diamonds and to transform our wounds into weapons of mass construction." The intricate beadwork evokes a sense of fragility, while simultaneously exuding a sense of power. According to Monnin, "The Resurrection Angel joins the Phoenix rising from the ashes." In Greek mythology, a phoenix ends its life cycle by burning into a pile of ashes from which a new phoenix arises. Similarly, *L'Ange de la Résurrection* is rising up from its difficult past, looking to the heavens with a hopeful, confident expression. Although she began creating this work in 2006, it was not completed and named *L'Ange de la Résurrection* until 2011 when the mobile became a symbol for new life after the 2010 earthquake.

- Katherine Mato

Prosper Pierre-Louis
b. 1947, Bainet, Haiti
d. 1997, Haiti

Prosper Pierre-Louis spent his childhood in the coastal town of Bainet in Haiti's southeast department and moved to Port-au-Prince at age sixteen. In the early 1970s he decamped to Soisson-la-Montagne, a mountain village near the capital, and helped form the Saint-Soleil (Holy Sun) peasant art collective initiated by Jean-Claude Garoute (Tiga) and Maud Robard. Pierre-Louis along with four other members — including Louisiane Saint Fleurant and Levoy Exil who are also featured in this exhibition — reorganized into the Cinq Soleils (Five Suns). Their techniques garnered admiration in Haiti and internationally, and Pierre-Louis is considered one of the most prominent members of the group. His flourishing career was cut short when he passed away suddenly in 1997.

21

Lavender Lwa, 1987
oil on canvas
23 5/8 x 19 1/2 in. (60 x 49.5 cm)
Gift of Dr. and Mrs. Bernard M. Wagner, 99.0014.01

22

Issa, not dated
acrylic on canvas
Sight: 23 5/8 x 11 5/8 in. (60 x 29.5 cm)
Framed: 27 5/8 x 15 5/8 x 2 in. (70.2 x 39.7 x 5.1 cm)
Gift of Anne Doniger, 2002.41.1

The son of an *oungan*, or Vodou priest, Pierre-Louis frequently utilized
Vodou imagery in his paintings. *Lavender Lwa* features several spirits.
Pierre-Louis often depicted *lwa* as amoebic beings floating through
space, as seen here. The serpent-like image found at the top of this
painting is also characteristic of his work, which incorporates aspects of
the natural world. *Issa* demonstrates Pierre-Louis's ability to combine
delicate cross-hatching with supreme use of color. The Saint-Soleil and
Cinq Soleils groups experimented with natural dyes created from beans,
seeds, and other plants found in the mountain landscape around them

in order to create new shades of color. The opulence and intricacy of detail demonstrate the spiritual exuberance of this work.

- Amelia Hintzen

23

Louisiane Saint Fleurant
b. 1924, Petit-Trou-de-Nippes, Haiti
d. 2005, Soisson-la-Montagne, Haiti
Untitled, 2004
acrylic on cloth
23 7/8 × 36 in. (60.6 × 91.4 cm)
Museum purchase, 2013.29
© 2004 Louisiane Saint Fleurant

Louisiane Saint Fleurant was a founding member of the Saint-Soleil (Holy Sun) art movement and later went on to form the Cinq Soleils (Five Suns) group, along with four male artists including Prosper Pierre-Louis and Levoy Exil, who are also featured in this exhibition. Saint Fleurant's work often depicts scenes of mothers, children, and the natural world. In this work painted in 2004, one year before she passed away, Saint Fleurant represents a mother with her two children. The mother is in the center, outfitted in what appears to be a white crocheted dress, while her children stand on either side of her, clothed in colorful garments. In the background are vibrant flowers with a variety of birds nestled amidst their foliage. The painting has a unique texture, which is created in part by the material on which it was painted. The acrylic sits atop a light curtain, its floral print seen on the painting's reverse.

- Katherine Mato

Sacha Tebó
b. 1934, Port-au-Prince, Haiti
d. 2004, Santiago, Dominican Republic

Sacha Thébaud, often referred to as Sacha Tebó, was raised and educated in Port-au-Prince and Montreal. He later studied architecture at the University of Miami and some of his earliest exhibitions were held in Miami galleries. Over the course of his career he lived and worked all

24

Le Mariage (The Wedding), 1962
pigments and wax on canvas
50 x 40 x 1 3/4 in. (127 x 101.6 x 4.4 cm)
Gift of the Artist, 66.114.000
© 1962 Sacha Tebó

over the Caribbean and Latin America, including in Haiti, the U.S. Virgin Islands, Mexico, Brazil, and the Dominican Republic. Tebó's art and architecture have been celebrated and exhibited across the region and he is often considered a pan-Caribbean artist. In addition to creating visual art, Tebó was a vocal advocate for improving urban design, infrastructure, and forest cover in Haiti and the Dominican Republic.

Tebó's works often contain references to Caribbean rhythm, movement, and color. Created early in his career, *Le Mariage* portrays colors and subjects that reflect Caribbean themes. The basic church interior, the couple's dress and appearance, and the landscape glimpsed through the window gesture to a Caribbean setting. Tebó's style in this work employs aspects of cubism. The painting utilizes a technique known as encaustics that Tebó began experimenting with at a young age and for which he later became known. This medium, originally developed in ancient Greece and Egypt, involves the application of pigmented beeswax to a canvas, adding texture and dimension to the scene.

During the early years of his career, Tebó experimented with cubist techniques. *Portrait of a Man* was created around the time Tebó was forced to flee Haiti for political reasons following the murder of his father-in-law by the forces of dictator François Duvalier. While this painting utilizes vibrant, warm colors typical of Tebó's work, it depicts a dejected figure cradling his head in his hands. The somber subject of the work conveys tension and anxiety.

- Amelia Hintzen

25

Portrait of a Man, 1963
pigments and wax on flour
sack
39 1/4 x 17 1/4 in. (99.7 x
43.8 cm)
Gift of Richard Levine,
84.0187

26   **Gérard Valcin**
b. 1925, Port-au-Prince, Haiti
d. 1988, Haiti
Brave Guede, ca. 1980
oil on canvas board
23 1/2 x 19 1/2 in. (59.7 x 49.5 cm)
Museum purchase through funds from Brian A. Dursum, 2004.388

After joining the Centre d'Art in the 1950s, Gérard Valcin decided to leave his job as a tile setter in order to pursue his artistic career full-time. Many of his works center on religious themes and in this painting Valcin depicts a member of the Gede family of *lwa*, who preside over death as well as birth, and are also identified with sex, humor, and children. This member of that important spirit family, Gede Brav, is identified with the Roman Catholic Saint Gerard Maiella who is often figured holding a crucifix with a skull positioned nearby. Valcin's Gede Brav is clothed in a hallmark dark suit and tall hat, inscribed with his name. Leaning on a bamboo cane, he kneels before a large cross signifying both the Christian crucifix and the spiritually powerful crossroads where, in Vodou, the living, the dead, and the spirit worlds meet. This multivalent symbolism is echoed in the crossed bones on the ground beneath him, in the decoration of libation bottles, and in the gravesite markers visible beyond the altar table.

- Katherine Mato and Kate Ramsey

27 **Pauleus Vital**
b. 1917, Jacmel, Haiti
d. 1984, Jacmel, Haiti
Ezili Je Wouj (Ezili of the Red Eyes), 1980
oil on masonite
28 7/8 x 24 in. (73.3 x 61 cm)
Gift of Dr. and Mrs. Bernard M. Wagner, 99.0014.02

Pauleus Vital was a shipbuilder and cabinetmaker in Jacmel before joining the Centre d'Art in Port-au-Prince in 1958. His half-brother Préfète Duffaut, already a well-established painter, encouraged him to pursue a career in the visual arts. In 1980, four years before his death, Vital painted *Ezili Je Wouj*, named for an emanation of the *lwa* Ezili Dantò, warrior woman and strongly protective single mother. In the middle of the painting stands a towering *mapou* tree, its branches morphing into hybrid beings, the central one with red eyes. The *mapou*'s trunk and roots create several defined ritual spaces in which initiates invite Ezili Je Wouj as well as the *lwa* Legba Kalfou and Gede by drawing their associated ritual diagrams, or *vèvè*, on the ground. The striking accents of red identify the ceremonies depicted in the painting with the Petwo family of *lwa*.

- Katherine Mato and Kate Ramsey

28

Frantz Zéphirin
b. 1968, Cap-Haïtien, Haiti
*Les Séquelles de la Colonisation (*The Legacies of Colonization), not dated
oil on canvas
23 1/4 x 19 1/4 in. (59.1 x 48.9 cm)
Museum purchase, 2000.026

Born into a family of distinguished painters, Frantz Zéphirin grew up observing his uncle Antoine Obin at work. He went on to develop his own distinctive style, a surrealism combining references to Vodou (he is an *oungan*, or priest), Catholicism, history, and geopolitics. Zéphirin encodes his work with social and political commentary, and *Les Séquelles de la Colonisation* reflects his particular interest in the allegorical representation of water creatures and animals more generally. Upon a background of animals with distinctly-drawn eyes (an iconographic motif of his work) float three hybrid beings. The figure on the left has the head of a rooster and body of a human, and that on the right combines the heads of a ram and a long-necked bird with a lobster claw and a fish tail. The jackets of two of the figures are adorned with epaulets and one wears a gendarme cap. In an artist's statement about this work, reflecting on the legacies of colonialism in Haitian society, Zéphirin writes that "the actors of the Haitian crisis metamorphize into wild animals so as to have their piece of the cake." Yet "in the end it is the people who suffer" while "the big neighbor [the United States] looks on without doing anything because in reality he is the great winner."

- Katherine Mato and Kate Ramsey

CONTRIBUTORS

CARLO A. CELIUS is a historian and art historian. He is a researcher for the Centre National de la Recherche Scientifique (CNRS, France) at the Institut des Mondes Africains (Paris). He is the author of *Langage plastique et énonciation identitaire: L'invention de l'art haïtien* (Les Presses de l'Université Laval, 2007). He edited *Le défi haïtien: Économie, dynamique sociopolitique et migration* (L'Harmattan, 2011), and *Situations créoles: Pratiques et représentations* (Éditions Nota Bene, 2006). He was the editorial coordinator for the following journal issues: "Création plastique, traites et esclavages" in *Cahiers des anneaux de la mémoire,* no. 12 (2009); "Haïti: face au passé / Haiti: Confronting the Past" in *Ethnologies* 28, no. 1 (2006); and "Haïti et l'anthropologie" in *Gradhiva,* nouvelle série, no. 1 (2005).

LOUIS HERNS MARCELIN is a faculty member and researcher in the Department of Anthropology and Department of Public Health Sciences at the University of Miami. He co-founded and is Chancellor of the Interuniversity Institute for Research and Development (INURED), a premiere research institution in Haiti. He has taught as a visiting scholar at the Universidade Federal do Rio de Janeiro, Brazil; Ecole Normale Supérieure, Paris, France; and Ecole Pratique des Hautes Etudes en Sciences Sociales, Université de Paris-Sorbonne. As a professor of social sciences at the University of Miami, he directs several large-scale studies on gang violence, HIV risk, and the increasing involvement of the juvenile justice system in the lives of Haitian adolescents and their families. His research interests include family, kinship, and migration; global health, disaster and recovery; and violence, politics, and generation in the Caribbean and Brazil.

PASCALE MONNIN was born in Port-au-Prince in 1974 and studied in Geneva, Switzerland. Swiss and Haitian, her dual culture has nourished a complex and enchanting imagination. She paints, sculpts, and engraves copper, and her art has taken her around the world. With James Noël, she founded the association Passengers of the Winds in 2010, which organizes artist residencies and cultural events. In 2012 they launched the artistic and literary review *IntranQu'illités.* She represented Haiti at the Venice Biennale in 2012 and exhibited in 2013 at the Villa Medici in Rome, at Agnès B in Paris, at the OAS Museum in Washington, D.C., and elsewhere. The Monnin Gallery, founded in Port-au-Prince in 1956, is a family business.

JERRY PHILOGENE is an Associate Professor in the American Studies Department at Dickinson College. In addition to exploring the intersections of race, ethnicity, class, and gender as articulated in contemporary visual arts, her research and teaching interests include interdisciplinary American cultural history, black cultural politics, and theories of diaspora and citizenship. She is currently working on a manuscript titled *The Socially Dead and the "Dead Citizen": Visuality and the Haitian Diaspora,* which provides a rich and textured analysis of the power of the visual field and its complex relationship to violence, domination, and liberation. Her published articles have appeared in *Small Axe: A Caribbean Journal of Criticism, BOMB Magazine, Radical History Review,* and most recently *MELUS: Multi-Ethnic Literature of the United States.*

KATE RAMSEY is a faculty member in the Department of History at the University of Miami. Her research interests include the politics of religion, law, and performance in the Caribbean and the Atlantic world; ideas of modernity and enchantment; and Caribbean intellectual history, artistic production, and social movements. Her award-winning first book *The Spirits and the Law: Vodou and Power in Haiti* (University of Chicago Press, 2011) examines the history and legacies of penal and ecclesiastical laws against popular ritual practices in Haiti. Ramsey's published articles have appeared in *Gradhiva, The Journal of Haitian Studies, Radical History Review, Transition Magazine,* and several edited volumes.

***

M. STEPHANIE CHANCY is a lecturer in Art History at Florida International University, where she is also a second year Ph.D. student in History. Her research focuses on cultural and social linkages between Europe and the French Caribbean, examining how these are reflected in the visual arts and especially portraiture.

JENNIFER GARCON is a Ph.D. student in the Department of History at the University of Miami. Her research centers on media and cultural politics in the Cold War Caribbean, focusing on Haiti.

AMELIA HINTZEN is an advanced Ph.D. student in the Department of History at the University of Miami. She studies the Dominican Republic and Haiti and her research interests include race, gender, and migration on Hispaniola.

KATHERINE MATO graduated from the University of Miami in 2013 and is a graduate student in the History of Art and Visual Culture at the University of Oxford.

HADASSAH ST. HUBERT is a Ph.D. student and McKnight Doctoral Fellow in the Department of History at the University of Miami. Her dissertation focuses on Haiti's participation in twentieth century world's fairs and expositions.

MUSEUM STAFF

YINA BALAREZO	Membership Coordinator
JULIE BERLIN	Registration Assistant
ANGELES CARDENAS	Receptionist
NATASHA CUERVO	Museum Registrar for Exhibitions and Loans
JILL DEUPI	Beaux Arts Director and Chief Curator
JANIE GRAULICH	Receptionist
ALESSIA LEWITT	Preparator
RAYMOND MATHEWS	Communications Specialist
MARIE MILHOMME	Chief Security Officer
DARREN PRICE	Senior Preparator
LORRIE STASSUN	Office Manager
JODI SYPHER	Curator of Education
HOPE TORRENTS	School Programs Coordinator
ADRIANA VERDEJA	Senior Director of Development